CHAPTER 1

PREPARING

IN THIS CHAPTER YOU WILL
LEARN ABOUT

- identifying the major types of research and research papers
- selecting a research topic that interests you and helps you contribute to the field of study you have chosen
- writing an effective thesis statement

Deliberate and sound decisions regarding your topic and thesis statement are vital to getting off to a good start on your research paper. They build the foundation for all that comes after, and they help ensure that you will spend a minimal amount of time later in the process revising these fundamental elements.

THE MAJOR TYPES OF RESEARCH AND RESEARCH PAPERS

In your graduate study you will most likely not conduct original research. Instead, you will probably review the research others have conducted and apply their findings to the topic you are studying. However, even though you will use research conducted by others, your finished paper should present *your own* thoughts, ideas, and arguments. This kind of research is still original in one sense: it is the outcome of your own careful evaluation of others' work and your own conclusions about the topic you are studying.

In this section we will briefly review the characteristics of standard academic research and describe two kinds of research papers.

TYPES OF RESEARCH

Research, according to *Webster's Unabridged Encyclopedic Dictionary of the English Language* (1996), is "diligent and systematic inquiry or investigation into a subject in order to discover or revise facts, theories, applications, etc."

There are two major types of research. The first type is primary research, in which a researcher conducts an original study to offer insight into a particular topic. For example, if your research question is "What is the extent of homelessness in the United States?" you might survey the directors of centers for the homeless in your community.

The second type of research is secondary research, in which the researcher compiles research conducted by others and applies it to new questions and/or theories. Most papers written for graduate courses are based on secondary research, and when we discuss research papers in this guide, we will be referring to papers of this type.

For example, you would conduct secondary research to answer a question such as "What factors contribute to homelessness in American society?" Answering this question would require you to review original studies of homelessness, gather and evaluate expert opinions about homelessness, and formulate your own conclusions.

THE PURPOSE OF A RESEARCH PAPER

The purpose of a research paper is to study a topic or issue in depth and share in writing what you discover. This kind of study not only helps you find solutions to the problems you are trying to solve, but also enables those who come after you to benefit from your hard work in the same way you benefit from the research done before yours.

It is important that you do not think of your paper as merely a book report in which you summarize what other people have said about an issue. Although that may be part of your research paper, what is more important is *your* contribution to the issue. You must think about and show how the research findings you have gathered can stimulate new ways of thinking about the issue.

TYPES OF RESEARCH PAPERS

Research papers may typically be categorized as either analytical or argumentative.

ANALYTICAL
In an analytical research paper, you perform research in order to become an expert on a topic so that you can restructure and present aspects of the topic from your own perspective ("Writer's Complex").

TABLE OF CONTENTS

ACKNOWLEDGMENTS

Introduction to Graduate Research and Writing

STEERING COMMITTEE

Sheila Berger, Lecturer Emerita, State University of New York at Albany;
PhD, English Literature, New York University

Carolyn Jarmon, Director of Graduate Studies, SUNY Empire State College;
PhD, Consumer Economics (Minor: Educational Evaluation), Cornell University

Meredyth A. Leahy, Dean of Liberal Arts, Regents College;
EdD, Adult Education, Temple University

Lawrence R. Reis, Director, External Master's Program, Skidmore College;
PhD, English, Southern Illinois University

AUTHORS

Nancy Engler, Director of Education, Sylvan Learning Center®;
MEd, Learning and Instructional Technology, Arizona State University

Lynn Oborn, Documentation Specialist, DA Consulting Group;
PhD, English (Rhetoric and Computer Composition), Southern Illinois University

Robert Yagelski, Director, Writing Center, State University of New York at Albany;
PhD, Rhetoric and Composition, The Ohio State University

EDITORS

Dan D'Allaird, Graduate Student Advisor, Regents College;
MA, English Language and Literature, University of Virginia

Lisa C. Zugner, Technical Writer/Researcher, Regents College;
BS, Journalism, West Virginia University

Writing is an integral and crucial part of your graduate study. As a graduate student, you will write not only to complete assignments but also to engage in in-depth inquiry within the subject areas you study. You will also write as a way to become a participant in the ongoing conversations about important issues within those subject areas. Your thoughts on a subject are useful to others to the extent that you communicate those thoughts effectively. Good writing accomplishes this, and thus it should be a major goal in your graduate study.

The purpose of this guide is to provide an overview of what is involved in completing a formal research paper at the graduate level. Since virtually all phases of your graduate study will include formal written papers based on your study of published sources, you will need to write good research papers to be successful in your graduate work. To do so, you will need to be familiar with the components of research papers and you will also need to be able to conduct research efficiently. You will, in short, need to engage in in-depth inquiry into the various subjects you study in your graduate program and write about them intelligently and thoroughly according to established conventions for research papers.

This guide will help you learn how to do that. It offers advice and suggestions for selecting a topic for your research, conducting research on that topic, locating and evaluating sources for your research, and writing and revising your research paper from rough draft to finished form.

The Appendixes contain lists of databases that you might consider using to help you locate material, a list of common reference works grouped by subject, and examples of Modern Language Association (MLA), American Psychological Association (APA), and Council of Biology Editors (CBE) style. (Note: Citations in this guide are made according to MLA-style guidelines.)

The steps involved in the research and writing process are presented sequentially in this guide. In practice, the process often involves many repeated steps and may feel more circular or winding than linear. You should be prepared for this as you undertake your research and writing project.

Many features in this guide are designed to make the material presented here accessible and easy to follow. One such feature is shaded boxes like the one you see on this page. These boxes present several different kinds of information: resources related to specific topics, reminders of ideas or concepts discussed in the guide, and general learning tips. In addition, the section titled "Additional Resources" at the end of each chapter points you to books and other resources that elaborate on points made in the guide.

This guide provides a great deal of advice and guidance. It is not, however, intended to make you an expert in any of the topic areas it covers. If you have serious reservations about your knowledge or understanding of anything presented within these pages, you should seek advice from your advisor/mentor about your concerns. As you read through the guide, you may find that you need to consult more detailed sources and/or seek assistance from experts such as librarians, professors, or tutors in a university writing center.

The guide is not meant to be a substitute for a writing handbook or grammar textbook. You should have such books at your disposal and consult them when necessary as you work through the guide. (You can find a list of such handbooks under the **Works Cited** heading on page 80.)

Research writing at the graduate level can be difficult and sometimes frustrating. However, it is an enormously powerful mode of inquiry and learning and, as such, it can be a satisfying and rewarding experience. This guide is intended to help you make your research writing the positive part of your graduate study that it can — and should — be.

For example, a student interested in adult developmental psychology may choose to examine the impact of long-term caregiving on the caregiver's view of self. You could break the topic down into two subtopics: the caregiver's duties and the caregiver's view of self. You could then research those subtopics in order to develop your general perspective and conclusions about the caregiver's role and view of self. Such research is really an extensive analysis of a problem or issue.

ARGUMENTATIVE

In an argumentative research paper you present your position on an issue. This type of paper is analytical, but it uses information as evidence to support a position ("Writer's Complex"). In some cases, you might begin conducting research knowing what you want to find out and then focus your energies on finding support for your position. This does not mean that you ignore research that contradicts what you're trying to support. Rather, you consider opposing viewpoints or information that contradicts your position and you attempt to address those viewpoints or contradictions. In some instances, in fact, your position may change as a result of your research. But in either case, the goal of an argumentative research paper is to support a stand on an issue.

For example, if your area of interest is the sociology of health care, you may wish to write a paper arguing that midwifery is a safe, viable alternative to hospital deliveries. In such a case you would present information that would demonstrate the safety of midwifery. You would also present arguments in favor of midwifery and address opposing viewpoints.

Notice that this is a very different focus than that of an analytical research paper. An analytical paper on midwifery, in contrast, might examine the practice in depth, presenting its shortcomings and benefits without making a case for or against the practice.

LITERATURE REVIEW

When you write a research paper, you build on what you know about a topic and what others have said or learned about that topic. You seek out information and expert opinion about the topic. The first step is to find out what is already known about your topic. To do so you conduct a literature review.

A literature review is a gathering and investigation of published material related to a research topic. Don't be surprised if, once you begin, you discover that there has been more written about your topic than you can read in the time available to you. You must determine which prior research findings are most relevant to your project. This involves making choices. Only very rarely will you be able to review all the available literature. (Chapter II: **Researching** discusses how to evaluate and select useful sources for your research.)

As you undertake your literature review, you will need to analyze the information you gather in order to apply it to the specific topic you are studying. This is the unique component that only you can bring to your research. In essence, you must evaluate what you find, consider opposing viewpoints or contradictory information, and apply your own insight to the issue at hand. Often, the act of conducting a literature review and synthesizing the material in the review will encourage you to reconsider an opinion you previously held or to adopt a different perspective on an issue. That is one of the primary purposes of engaging in research: to gain a deeper understanding of an issue or topic.

Keep in mind that conducting a literature review, however, is more than simply gathering relevant information. As explained in the following pages, you are trying to support a thesis or answer a question. Searching the available literature is thus part of your study of that thesis or question, your inquiry into the topic you are studying in depth.

> *An argument uses evidence to take a stand on an issue, whereas analysis uses evidence to examine a topic thoroughly. While argumentative and analytical research papers differ in this fundamental way, virtually all of the writing and research principles discussed in this guide apply to both of them. As you consider these principles, you should adapt them to fit your individual style and the type of paper you are writing.*

SELECTING A RESEARCH TOPIC

Sometimes the most difficult part of conducting research is selecting a good topic. However, if you are to write an effective paper, it is crucial that you select your topic carefully so that it is sufficiently narrow at the same time that it provides you with fertile ground for in-depth research. One of the most common mistakes students make when writing research papers is selecting topics that are too broad to be addressed adequately in conventional research papers. A good way to avoid this problem and focus your research is to frame your topic as a question.

THE RESEARCH QUESTION

Since the point of research is to study a topic in depth and share what you discover, it may be a good idea to think of your topic in terms of a carefully worded question. Writing an effective research paper depends a great deal on asking the right question. A good research question can be narrowed or broadened, calls for an answer, and is interesting to you and to your advisor. It should grow out of your study in a particular subject or discipline and should be significant within the field you are studying. Ideally, it is a question that, when answered well, will contribute to your own as well as to others' understanding of that field.

For example, imagine you are studying the history of ethics and science and you are specifically interested in the relationship between religious belief and the rise of modern science. You might, then, consider the following research questions for a paper:

- How did Darwin's *The Origin of Species* affect the relationship between the scientific community and organized religion?

- How did the reaction to Darwin's theories among clerics influence the development of modern biology and its acceptance outside the scientific community?

- How did the opposition to Darwin's theories by organized religion contribute to the eventual widespread acceptance of Darwin's theory of natural selection?

Notice that the first two questions would likely lend themselves to analytical papers, whereas the third question implies a specific point of view regarding Darwin's theories that would lend itself to an argumentative paper. Obviously, both kinds of papers would require analysis, but a paper based on the third question would also require the writer to argue for the validity of a particular point of view regarding the relationship between the acceptance of Darwin's theories and the opposition of organized religion to his theories at that time.

The important point here is that your research question will inevitably shape the paper you write, so it is critical that you frame your question carefully.

It is also important to keep in mind that when we ask a question, we want an answer. A good research question should elicit a response such as "Hmmm . . . I don't know, but I think it's important to find out." The "I don't know" part of the response is important: if you already know the answer, then you would not really be engaged in genuine research. The "it's important to find out" part of the response is important, too: the last thing you want (or your reader wants) is a paper that elicits the dreaded "So what?" response.

> *In analytical papers, your research question will determine the type of information you seek. In argumentative papers, your response to your research question is your thesis statement, the position you will defend and support in the paper.*

Ultimately, the framing of a good question leads to a good research project. Using the question as a point of departure, you can see more easily what data you'll need to gather, what information you'll need to collect, what kinds of sources you'll need to consult, and what criteria for success you'll need to formulate.

DEVELOPING THE RESEARCH QUESTION

A good research question can emerge from your consultation of a variety of sources: your study of a particular topic or issue, something a colleague or your professor said about an issue that sparks your interest and invites you to explore further, something you read that leads you to further questioning, discussions within groups on the Internet, and/or your own knowledge of a subject or field.

When you identify a potential topic, write down a list of questions that you would like to answer. For example, let's say that you decide to research how U.S. corporate decisions impact politics in Middle Eastern countries. You might consider the following questions for your paper:

- How many Middle Eastern countries have elected leaders from emerging political parties?

- How do international relations affect Middle Eastern politics?

- How have the actions of U.S. corporations affected the political relations between the U.S. and Middle Eastern countries?

Now evaluate each question, considering the following:

IS THE QUESTION FOCUSED AND WELL-DEFINED?

The first question is obviously too narrow. It would not lend itself to the kind of in-depth examination and analysis that you would be expected to do for a graduate-level research paper. You could reasonably answer the question with minimal research that focuses simply on the results of elections in these countries. A reader might legitimately ask, "Why is this important?"

By contrast, the second question is too broad. To answer such a question adequately would require an enormous amount of inquiry into the broad and complicated area of international relations. At best, you would be able to offer only a very general and superficial answer to such a question in a conventional research paper. Such a question more reasonably lends itself to a book-length project. Clearly, the scope of such a project goes well beyond a conventional research paper.

The third question is a better question for a graduate-level research paper. Its scope is manageable, but it addresses a subject that is clearly complex enough to support in-depth research. It also suggests the types of data you will need to gather and the types of sources you might logically consult. Such a question will guide your research in ways that the other two questions cannot.

DOES THE QUESTION HAVE RESEARCH POTENTIAL?

Consider whether the question lends itself to in-depth research that will lead to an adequate answer. In the example above, the third question clearly invites such inquiry.

THE RESEARCH PLAN

A research plan is a written layout of the kinds of information, data, and arguments that you will need to gather to answer your research question.

To formulate a research plan you should determine whether you have adequate access to resources to answer the question. Do a quick preliminary search in a journal index, electronic databases, a library catalog, or other appropriate sources to determine how much information is available and whether the available materials will enable you to explore your question adequately.

If you determine that the appropriate source material is available to you, you should then consider what will be involved in answering your question. In other words, what ideas or arguments will you need to explore?

For example, if you formulated a research question such as "Are corporations in Norway more successful than corporations in Hungary?" you would first need to define what "more successful" means before addressing the issue of whether corporations find more success in Norway. To do so would likely require that you investigate what economists and other experts have to say about how to determine corporate "success." Second, you would need to look more closely at the differences and similarities between the economies of Norway and Hungary, which would most likely require you to look into the histories and cultures of those two nations. You would also need to find out which corporations do business in those nations. Finally, you would need to determine whether those corporations meet your criteria for "success."

In short, before you take your first note for your paper, you must identify precisely what information you will need to gather from your sources.

PRACTICE EXERCISE

CONSIDERING THE OPTIONS

The following questions were developed by the Empire State College Writer's Complex (1995-1996) and may be helpful for evaluating the quality of your research question. You might use this question as a sample: "How have the actions of corporations in the United States affected the political relations between the United States and Middle Eastern countries?" Or you may use the space below to write your own question.

_____

_____

_____

_____

_____

_____

_____

1. Does the question deal with a topic or issue that interests me enough to spark my own thoughts and opinions?

2. Is the question easily and fully researchable?

3. What type of information do I need to answer the research question (statistics, financial data, government documents, reports, research)?

4. Can I access these sources?

5. Does the question cover a reasonable time frame?

6. Given the type and scope of the information that I need, is my question too broad, too narrow, or just right?

7. Do I have a high-quality question that I will actually be able to answer by doing research?

After reviewing these questions, you might consider narrowing the research question to "How have the actions of corporations in the United States affected the political relations between the United States and Middle Eastern countries since the 1967 Middle East War?" This question narrows the scope of the topic to 30 years. Your review of available literature may lead you to narrow the question even further to apply to specific Middle Eastern countries or to specific actions of U.S. corporations.

How would you modify your own research question? Rewrite it in the space below.

_____

_____

_____

_____

_____

_____

Writing an Effective Thesis Statement

A thesis statement is a proposed answer to a research question. It is the basic stand you take, the opinion you express, and the point you make about your subject. You should articulate your thesis concisely and explicitly in a few sentences at most. The statement should let your reader know exactly what position you are supporting. It should be narrow enough to be developed thoroughly within the framework of your paper.

In most cases, you will present your thesis statement in the introductory section of your paper. Your introduction may be a paragraph, several paragraphs, or even a few pages in length. Within that space, you should present your thesis clearly so that your reader knows where you are headed in your paper.

CHARACTERISTICS OF AN EFFECTIVE THESIS STATEMENT

An effective thesis statement has several characteristics.

- It is **specific**. If your ideas are unclear or vague, your paper will probably be the same. Even though you can define and expand on general terms later in the text, your thesis statement should be clear and unambiguous.

- It is **restrictive**. If you try to cover large topic areas with your thesis, your paper may be too long or, worse, it may be vague, general, or superficial. When you restrict the size and scope of your topic, your project will be more manageable and your paper will likely be more specific, in-depth, and efficient.

- It is **compelling**. It engages your readers and inspires them to read further. It holds interest for those with knowledge of the field. It conveys the significance of your research project.

- It is also implicitly **referential**. Your thesis is the result of your careful study and analysis of a topic or issue. As a result, it is inherently connected to the field you are studying and it refers implicitly (and sometimes explicitly) to that field.

A thesis statement serves an important function for your reader. It is an indication of what you will try to prove in your paper and what the reader is likely to encounter in the paper. It is a kind of promise on which you will deliver.

A thesis statement also serves an important function for you. It focuses your research and guides you as you explore your topic. It is important to keep in mind that initially, your thesis statement is tentative. As you conduct your research and explore the issue you're writing about, you may find that you need to revise your thesis statement.

PRACTICE EXERCISE

CONSIDERING THE OPTIONS

Referring to the thesis statement characteristics discussed earlier in this chapter, evaluate the following thesis statements for a proposed research paper on the sociology of health care. Try to determine how well each of these statements incorporates the characteristics and consider how each might be revised to be more effective.

1. More families participate in managed health care plans than in traditional health insurance plans.

2. Cost containment measures by managed health care organizations will decrease the overall quality of health care in America.

3. In order to maintain a high quality of health care in America, managed health care organizations should be required to publicize their cost-containment policies.

4. Health care is a problem that must be addressed in this country.

Analyzing Your Responses

Statement one ("More families participate in managed health care plans than in traditional health insurance plans.") is essentially a statement of fact. It is certainly **specific** and **restrictive**, but it would not be **compelling** to readers with knowledge of the issue since it does not imply a stance or indicate the need for an in-depth examination of an issue or problem. It also does not make a statement that implicitly refers to problems or issues that others have explored or argued about regarding health care, and thus it is not sufficiently **referential**.

Statement two ("Cost containment measures by managed health care organizations will decrease the overall quality of health care in America.") has the potential to be developed into a good argumentative research paper. It is adequately **specific** and **restrictive**, although it is somewhat broad and may require narrowing as the research is conducted. Unlike the first statement, it is **compelling** in that it indicates a stance that relates to an important issue in the field of health care (maintaining quality while controlling costs). In this sense, it is also sufficiently **referential**.

Statement three ("In order to maintain a high quality of health care in America, managed health care organizations should be required to publicize their cost-containment policies.") is more **specific** and **restrictive** than statement two and states quite clearly what the author's position and focus of the paper will be. Like statement two, it is **compelling** in that it addresses an issue of interest to those concerned and knowledgeable about health care. It is also clearly **referential** in that it implicitly refers to policies that have been the focus of debate among health care experts. This would be a good thesis statement.

Statement four ("Health care is a problem that must be addressed in this country.") is not at all **specific** or **restrictive**; rather, it is far too general and even vague to inspire the writer to sufficiently focus the research project. It may be mildly **compelling,** but not compelling enough to engage the interest of knowledgeable readers. It is not **referential;** instead, it merely makes a generalization with which most people would probably concur. This statement is a poor thesis statement that would likely lead to a vague and superficial research paper.

ADDITIONAL RESOURCES

Hacker, Diana. *The Bedford Handbook for Writers*. 5th ed. Boston: Bedford, 1998.

Hult, Christine. *Research and Writing in the Humanities*. Needham Heights: Allyn & Bacon, 1996.

Lamm, Kathryn. *10,000 Ideas for Term Papers, Projects, Reports, and Speeches*. 4th ed. Indianapolis: Arco, 1995.

Markman, Roberta, et al. *10 Steps in Writing the Research Paper*. 5th ed. Hauppauge: Barrons, 1994.

For links to dozens of additional online writing centers and resources, visit http://www.ume.maine.edu/~wcenter/others.html.

There are also many resources for writers on the World Wide Web (which will be discussed further in the following chapters). Here are a few of them:

The Online Writery at the University of Missouri
http://www.missouri.edu/~writery
Includes many resources and features for writers.

The Purdue University Online Writing Lab
http://owl.english.purdue.edu
Includes help documents and many links to related sites.

The Writer's Complex at Empire State College
http://www.esc.edu/htmlpages/writer/vwcmen.htm
Includes help documents and related resources.

The Writing Center at the State University of New York at Albany
http://www.albany.edu/~writing
Includes links to many useful online sites related to writing and to similar resources for online research.

CHAPTER II

RESEARCHING

IN THIS CHAPTER YOU WILL
LEARN ABOUT

• locating sources

• evaluating and selecting sources

• conducting a search using access tools

Your research paper demands more from you than
a listing of commonly known facts or opinions. It
demands investigation into facts and opinions that
are not commonly known. Research is your access to
these facts and opinions. It expands your knowledge
by adding depth and nuance to what you already
know about your research topic, and it reveals
aspects of that topic that were not previously
known to you.

LOCATING SOURCES

The types of sources of information available to you for your research are virtually limitless. They include academic, public, and state libraries; people (including library personnel and subject-matter experts); bookstores; government organizations; historical, literary, and other societies; museums; and the Internet. This section describes some of these sources and offers tips on how to use them well.

LIBRARIES

Libraries have changed a great deal in the last several years. Most sources that you will need for your paper are now available "on line," which means that they are available electronically, via a computer. Many sources that were formerly not available at all to the general public or that required lengthy waiting periods to obtain are now accessible almost instantly. This makes conducting research both easier and more difficult, easier in that more sources are available to you in one place and more difficult in that you must be able to evaluate these sources quickly to avoid becoming bogged down while doing your research.

ACADEMIC LIBRARIES

If you are enrolled in a course at a college or university, you should have full access to the institution's library and all of its services. If you are not enrolled in a course, you may still have access to the library and its reference tools. However, you will probably not be able to check out books or take advantage of interlibrary loan services (services in which a library borrows materials for its patrons from other libraries).

PUBLIC LIBRARIES

You may already make use of your public library for research or for entertainment. But did you know that your public library is also a source for interlibrary loan services? That is, if you need a source that your public library does not have, you can identify a library that does have the source and your library can borrow it for you. Policies regarding interlibrary loan vary from library to library. Check with your librarian for details.

STATE LIBRARIES

Many states have excellent state libraries that residents of those states may use. Many state library collections contain more scholarly journals than do public libraries. Many also have online catalogs that you can search from your home computer via modem connection. If you identify a book or article that you want, your state library may have it or be able to get it for you through interlibrary loan.

THE INTERNET

An internet is a linked group of computer networks. The Internet so commonly used and referred to today is the largest such internet in the world. It is a global web of national, regional, and local computer networks, and it grows literally every day. The Internet's many features include electronic mail, the transferring of files from one computer to another, and access to mailing lists and discussion groups. It is one of the most powerful tools available to a researcher.

The resources available through the Internet are vast and change rapidly, as do the ways you can access and navigate the Internet. For these reasons and others, you should consult one of the many Internet reference sources before you begin to use the Internet for your research. Several such reference sources are listed in "Additional Resources" at the end of this chapter.

Access to the Internet is available at many libraries and at home if you have a computer, a modem, and an Internet service provider. The Internet contains, quite literally, a world of resources. Descriptions of some of these resources follow.

ERIC RESOURCES
(http://www.aspensys.com/eric/index.html)

The Educational Resources Information Center (ERIC) database provides access to education-related literature. ERIC is available at many public and academic libraries as well as on the Internet. It provides document delivery for a fee. (Call the ERIC Document Reproduction Service at 1-800-443-ERIC for price and ordering information.) ERIC also maintains 16 subject-specific clearinghouses.

ERIC database listings include many different types of documents, including published articles, abstracts, and conference papers and proceedings, among others. These documents will likely not all be of equal value to you. For example, conference papers and proceedings can be more readable and informal than articles published in journals or books, but they may lack the detailed bibliographic information frequently contained in journal articles and books. As you conduct more and more research you will become increasingly skilled at evaluating the quality of your sources. (See Chapter III: **Reading** for more detailed information about evaluating your sources.)

For more information about ERIC, visit its World Wide Web site or call ERIC at 1-800-LET-ERIC and ask for a copy of *A Pocket Guide to ERIC*.

DOCUMENT DELIVERY SERVICES
Document delivery services provide you with paper copies of material you or the document delivery service locates on the Internet and elsewhere. Some services make their material available for free, while others make their material available on a "for-a-fee" basis. The following are a few of the document delivery services accessible on the Internet. Each service sets its own rates and policies.

- **CARL UnCover**
  http://www.charweb.org/education/carl.htm
  CARL UnCover is a table of contents database. You may search the database for free; however, there is a charge for ordering documents.
- **UMI InfoStore**
  http://www.umi.com/infostore
  UMI InfoStore allows you to order journal articles for a fee. You must have complete and accurate bibliographical information to order articles.
- **EBSCOdoc**
  http://www.ebscodoc.com
  This is a document delivery service that charges a fee for its services. Subscribers may search the database and order documents.
- **Kessler-Hancock**
  http://www.mother.com/~khinfo
  This company will conduct searches for you and deliver the documents to you for a fee.
- **KD Document**
  http://www.covesoft.com/KD_Document
  Same type of service as Kessler-Hancock.

As you search the sources discussed in this section, keep in mind that you should conduct your search with your research question as a guide. Don't simply go out and find sources that seem interesting. Rather, focus on the sources that you have already determined might prove most promising in providing the kinds of data you will need.

Selecting and Evaluating Sources

The kinds of sources you use to gather information, form ideas and opinions about your topic, and make and support your arguments are critical to the quality of your research paper. If you use poor or questionable sources, your final paper will reflect this. If, on the other hand, you use reliable and valid sources for your research, your final paper will be much stronger.

Types of Sources

Sources of information may be categorized as primary or secondary sources.

Primary sources are original, first-hand documents such as creative works, research studies, diaries, letters, and personal interviews.

Secondary sources are comments about or analyses of primary sources. They include analyses of creative works or research studies and interpretations of diaries, letters, or events.

You will likely use both primary and secondary sources to investigate your research question.

For example, suppose your research question is "How has the experience of Vietnamese immigrants in the United States differed from the experience of Chinese immigrants?" In this instance, personal interviews, autobiographies, and diaries by Vietnamese and Chinese immigrants would qualify as primary sources. An article in a magazine comparing the experiences based on writings by actual immigrants would qualify as a secondary source.

Reference Tools

A reference tool is a print or electronic document that is itself a source of information. It may also contain an access tool such as an index to help you gain access to information within the document itself. Some common types of reference tools are discussed below. For a subject list of reference tools, refer to Appendix B: **Common Reference Works**.

Almanacs and Yearbooks
Almanacs are compilations of statistical, tabular, and general data. An annually published almanac is sometimes called a yearbook. Use almanacs and yearbooks to get information such as demographic facts and figures. Sometimes almanacs can also be used to verify established trends or to compare data over time.

Biographies
Biographies are depictions of the lives of individuals. Use biographies to get background information about people involved in your area of research focus.

Books
Books provide a more comprehensive treatment of your research question than do articles or reports. Be aware, however, that by the time a book appears in print, the information within it is several years old. Use books to obtain the most thorough information about your topic.

Chronologies
Chronologies are written arrangements of events in order of occurrence. They place events on a timetable. Use chronologies to help you consider your research question or thesis in a time frame as it relates to other events.

COMPILATIONS

Compilations are collections of information about a single topic. They present, in one source, many significant documents or texts related to a research question or group of questions. Use compilations to gain an overview of your topic.

DICTIONARIES

Dictionaries are reference books which list words alphabetically and discuss their meanings, etymologies, and usages. Dictionaries may be either general English-language dictionaries or specialized works such as thesauruses or subject or foreign language dictionaries. Use dictionaries to define and determine correct spelling and usage of key words used in your field of investigation.

DIRECTORIES

Directories are organized lists of people or organizations. They contain information such as names, addresses, phone numbers, job titles, etc. The most commonly used directory is the telephone book. Use directories to get names, addresses, titles, and phone numbers of people or organizations you want to reference or to interview.

ENCYCLOPEDIAS

Encyclopedias present information from all branches of knowledge or from a single subject area and organize such data alphabetically for easy reference. In addition, many encyclopedias that are available in an electronic format provide links to related information. Use encyclopedias as a starting point for research on unfamiliar topics, for they offer concise summaries and, frequently, suggestions for further reading.

GEOGRAPHIC SOURCES

Geographic sources are documents such as maps and atlases. Use geographic sources to help you locate physical, economic, social, political, and demographic information pertinent to your research.

GOVERNMENT DOCUMENTS

Government documents include records of foreign and U.S. federal, state, and local government administrations, research documents, annual reports of government agencies, census data, and congressional records. Use government documents to learn about the activities of a government, obtain data collected by government agencies, investigate how government works, and research other information about foreign and U.S. federal, state, and local governments.

HANDBOOKS AND MANUALS

Handbooks and manuals are ready-reference sources that provide information relevant to particular, narrowly focused fields of knowledge. Some contain instructions or "how-to" advice. Use handbooks and manuals to gain information about the workings of organizations and/or procedures and instructions for a variety of tasks.

ACCESS TOOLS

Access tools are resources that direct you to other resources. Unlike reference tools, which contain information that is useful in and of itself, access tools serve the sole purpose of pointing you to other information sources. Several of the more common access tools are discussed below.

BIBLIOGRAPHIES

Bibliographies are listings of sources pertaining to particular topics. Academic libraries frequently prepare bibliographies of sources available in those libraries which provide information on research topics. Published bibliographies can also serve as guides to reference tools on particular topics.

INDEXES AND ABSTRACTS

Indexes are lists of information, topics, or references available in a publication. Indexes in books list the contents of the book in alphabetical order by topic. Indexes of periodicals list the contents of the periodicals for a specified time period.

Indexes can lead you to information in many different sources within your research area. For example, an index of business periodicals allows you to search for information on particular business topics. The list of sources in the index includes titles of many business-related journals.

Abstracts are concise summaries of published sources. They are usually grouped by topic. They are particularly useful in indexes, where they can provide information on the relevance of a source to your research needs.

Most indexes and abstracts are available in both print and electronic form. Print indexes and abstracts are usually located in library reference sections. Electronic indexes are available on CD-ROM and/or on line.

Electronic indexes and abstracts offer specific advantages over their print counterparts. First, they are updated frequently and usually cover at least three to five years of material. Second, they offer easier, speedier searching in that you may search by keying in specific words pertaining to your topic. One disadvantage to electronic indexes and abstracts is that they often don't go back as far in time as do print indexes.

LIBRARY CATALOGS

A library catalog is a written or electronic enumeration and description of the holdings of a library. It is probably the most familiar access tool you will find in the library. It provides specific information about the holdings of the library and/or the system that library belongs to. Some library catalogs only include information about books, while others provide information about journals, microfiche, audio, video, CD-ROM holdings, and more. Most library catalogs are now electronic, making the search process much faster and easier for library users.

PERIODICALS

There are three main types of periodicals: journals, magazines, and newspapers.

JOURNALS

Journals contain research reports, articles, book reviews, and interviews. They are the periodicals that you will probably use most often to search for answers to your research question. You will find the following types of information in journals:

- **Research reports:** These are reports of original research, a primary source of information. You can recognize research reports because they typically contain the following sections:
  - **Introduction:** Includes a thesis statement or research question.
  - **Method:** Describes the method used to conduct the research.
  - **Report:** Communicates the results of the research.
  - **Discussion:** Discusses the implications of the results.

A brief, informative guide to the benefits of many of the sources discussed here can be found at http://www.webnets.com/future/fu01080.htm. *Note that all of the indexes discussed in this site are listed in Appendix A: Academic Databases.*

- **Review articles:** Review articles are formal, written evaluations of one or more publications. Review articles are useful secondary sources. They can help you define your research question, provide information about the state of current research related to your research question, help you find relationships, gaps, or inconsistencies in the literature, and suggest ideas for further research or ways to solve a research problem.

- **Theoretical articles:** Theoretical articles are papers which draw upon existing literature to advance new theories or to analyze existing theories.

- **Book reviews:** Book reviews are evaluations of the contents of books. Book reviews in journals are usually written by experts in the subjects the books address. Most reviews compare a book to others on the same subject(s) and to others the author has written. Reviews are excellent sources for expert opinion about particular books.

- **Interviews:** Interviews are conversations in which information is obtained by one person from another. Interviews that appear in a journal are typically conducted with a subject expert by a member of the journal's editorial board.

MAGAZINES

Magazines contain mostly short articles by a variety of authors. You will find the following types of information in magazines:

- news stories

- editorials

- columns

- feature stories

- reviews

- interviews

Magazines are published in a wide variety of styles and formats, and the depth and quality of their information varies. The *Readers Guide to Periodical Literature* and other similar publications index articles from many popular magazines; indexes to scholarly journals are also available.

NEWSPAPERS

Newspapers are published frequently, usually daily, weekly, or semiweekly, and they tend to contain information that provides answers to the questions Who? What? When? Where? and Why? You will find the following types of information in newspapers:

- news stories

- editorials

- columns

- feature stories

- reviews

- announcements

Newspapers are a useful source for current, and frequently local, information. Sometimes you can obtain primary source information in newspapers.

There are several ways you can draw upon expert knowledge relevant to your research question. One way is to conduct personal interviews. Another is to check the bibliographies in articles and books you have read for the names of individuals who are cited and then to search for works written by or about those people. Yet another way is to participate in Internet discussion groups, where many experts share information. You may also communicate with experts via electronic mail — a sort of virtual interview.

INTERNET SOURCES

There is a great deal of information available on the Internet, and you can access most of it from your home computer at your convenience. You can read government, academic, professional, and private sector documents, search the ERIC database, search full-text electronic journals, and participate in discussion groups and e-mail conversations with experts and peers on line.

Because the Internet provides so much information, it can be difficult to locate exactly what you want or need. Some tools, however, can help you. The Internet's search engines are in many cases the best places to begin your online research.

SEARCH ENGINES

Search engines are computer programs that search for keywords in files and documents on the World Wide Web. Each search engine retrieves information from different sources. Which one or several will be most helpful to you will depend on the type of information you are looking for and how you want to access it. Until you become familiar with the particular features of each search engine, you should try as many of them as you can.

Following are several of the most commonly used search engines.

- **Alta Vista**
  http://www.altavista.digital.com
- **Excite**
  http://www.excite.com
- **HotBot**
  http://www.hotbot.com
- **InfoSeek**
  http://www.infoseek.com
- **Lycos**
  http://www.lycos.com
- **OpenText**
  http://www.opentext.net
- **WebCrawler**
  http://www.webcrawler.com

Some search engines also function as directories. They are organized by subject, and many contain bibliographies that might help you find information not identified by the search engine's queries of the World Wide Web. Following are some of the most commonly used directories.

- **The Argus Clearinghouse Net**
  http://www.clearinghouse.net
- **Magellan**
  http://www.mckinley.com
- **Virtual Reference Desk**
  http://thorplus.lib.purdue.edu/reference/index.html
- **World Wide Web Virtual Library**
  http://vlib.stanford.edu/Overview.html
- **Yahoo**
  http://www.yahoo.com

For quick access to several of the search engines listed here, visit http://www.colosys.net/search. *Use the tips found at this site to help make your searching fast and easy.*

Searching Electronic Databases Using Access Tools

As described in the section "Selecting and Evaluating Sources," access tools are resources that direct you to other resources. A database is a collection of information organized for rapid research and retrieval. Access tools that search electronic databases are frequently found in a database format. Searching electronic databases with access tools is quickly becoming the most common method of conducting academic research. Because using these access tools requires unique skills and information, this section is devoted exclusively to a discussion of searching electronic databases.

CHARACTERISTICS OF DATABASES

Most databases are limited to one academic discipline, and many disciplines have more than one useful database. You should identify the databases most likely to be helpful in your area of study. Any expert in your area of study may help you here. Once you identify these databases, use the following questions to determine which databases will probably be the most useful to you.

SCOPE
How broad is the database? Consider the following:

- subject areas it covers
- types of sources it includes (e.g., journal articles, essays, conference proceedings, newspaper articles, etc.)
- time frame it covers

SIZE
How large is the database? Look at the

- number of records it holds
- number of sources it indexes

STRUCTURE AND ACCESS
How is the database structured and how can you gain access to it and search through it? Determine the

- ways in which the information in the database is structured
- information that is searchable — typically, you can search author, title, subject, keyword, and descriptor (a significant word or phrase used to categorize or describe text or other material)

SEARCH METHODS
How are you be able to search the database? The two most common methods are

- free text searching, in which the database lists every instance of the use of a word or words that you key in
- controlled vocabulary searching, in which you search the database using a limited set of terms listed in the introductory material of the database

CURRENCY
- frequency of updates

QUALITY

Is the database valid and accurate? Consider the following:

• who takes responsibility for maintaining the database

• quality control practiced by the vendor

HELP

In the context of a computer database, help is a feature that offers assistance in using the database. Help is usually offered both in print and on line by the database provider.

ACCESS POINTS

An access point is a word or phrase shared by two or more entries in a database. Searching the database for the term generates a list of all the entries that contain that term. For example, a library catalog or database may list records by author. In such a case, the author's name is your access point to the works listed in the database that are written by that author.

Access points vary from database to database and from library catalog to library catalog. The most basic access points include

• **title**

• **author**

• **keyword** (a significant word or term from a title or document used as a search term in an Internet query)

• **subject** (All topics in a database fit into one or more subject areas. Using the subject as an access point may lead you to the topics included in that subject area. For example, searching for the subject "psychology" might yield topics such as "Jungian," "cognitive," "Freudian," and others.)

FORMULATING YOUR QUERY

To determine the access points in a database, you formulate a query. A query is an inquiry that seeks authoritative information. A query may take many forms including a question or a one-word statement. Each database describes the types of queries it responds to.

The aim of your query is to find answers to your research question. To do that, you need to break your question down into terms that you can use to search for information. Here are some steps to follow.

• Break your question down into concepts that can be searched separately and then connected.

• Decide how broad you want the search to be. (Do you want to retrieve as many documents as possible or gather a focused collection of information?)

• Select appropriate terms if the database uses a controlled vocabulary.

• Decide how you will limit your search to specific fields by shortening or narrowing the search.

EVALUATING YOUR SEARCH

Did your search result in finding relevant information? Did you find too much or too little information? First, look at your results to determine whether the information you retrieved is relevant to your topic. If not, your search may have been too broad, you may have selected the wrong database in which to search, you may have formulated your search incorrectly, or you may have just made a typographical error in your query.

If your search retrieved too much information but the information is relevant, try to limit your search to the current or last three years, or limit it to certain types of documents such as journal articles. (Some indexes list conference proceedings and book chapters as well as journal articles.)

If you retrieved too few documents, evaluate the scope of your search. If you determine that the scope is too narrow, broaden it. If you determine that the scope is appropriate but you are still not finding what you need, you may be searching an inappropriate database.

SEARCHING HINTS

Electronic indexes are produced by many publishers, each with its own software, search techniques, and structure. Each index you use will probably look unique. Always take time to look around the computer screen for reference to "help," "commands," or "getting started." These terms should lead you to online help. Also, if you are using a database at a library, look for a tip sheet near the computer. Many libraries place user instructions next to each public use computer.

KEYWORD VS. SUBJECT SEARCHING

Keyword and subject searching are similar, but their methodologies differ enough that each is useful in certain circumstances. For example, keyword searches are often the better choice when you search a database that uses a controlled vocabulary. If you don't know the subject under which your topic is classified, do a keyword search first. Then browse through the documents you retrieve to determine what topics are assigned. Conduct your subject search using those subject descriptors.

On the other hand, if you know the subject that includes your topic, it is usually advisable to begin your search there, as each document you retrieve will be directly relevant. You should be able to access the subject terms in either a thesaurus or an index provided in the database.

FREE TEXT SEARCHING

Free text searching is what you will do if you search the World Wide Web using an index such as OpenText. You will enter a word or several words and the search engine will search all documents containing those words that are available to it on the World Wide Web.

SEARCHING WITH BOOLEAN OPERATORS

Boolean operators are connecting words such as "AND," "OR," or "BUT" that establish a relationship between search terms. They can be used to narrow searches to retrieve the most relevant information.

Use the word **AND** to search for documents that include all terms linked by **AND** in your keyword search.

For example, a search on the phrase "labor relations AND Detroit" will retrieve all documents in which the terms "labor relations" and "Detroit" appear.

Use **OR** to search for documents that include *any* of the terms being linked by **OR** in your keyword search.

For example, a search on the phrase "labor relations OR Detroit" will retrieve all documents in which at least one of the terms appears in each of the documents retrieved.

Use **NOT** before specific terms in your keyword search to eliminate documents containing those terms. Using **NOT** in your keyword search reduces the number of documents retrieved.

For example, a search on the phrase "labor relations NOT Detroit" will retrieve all documents in which the term "labor relations" appears but the term "Detroit" does not appear.

TRUNCATION

Truncation is the use of a wild card (see below) or other symbol to shorten a term in an electronic search. Truncation is particularly useful if you are searching for variants of a root word.

For example, you may want to search for records containing the terms "intelligence," "intelligent," and "intelligentsia." Use the truncation feature to search for all three of the terms by entering *intelligen?* The question mark, in this case, is the truncation symbol. The symbol varies from publisher to publisher. Consult the online help feature to find out what the truncation symbol is for each specific database.

WILD CARD

A wild card is a symbol used in electronic searching which stands for any letter.

For example, if you are searching for an author named *Anderson* or *Andersen* but you aren't sure of the spelling, you can enter a wild card to retrieve both spellings. The wild card term would look something like this: *Anders*n.* The symbol varies from publisher to publisher; consult the online help to find out what it is for each particular database.

PRACTICE EXERCISE

CONSIDERING THE OPTIONS

Place an "X" next to the three sources that would probably yield the most relevant information to support the following thesis statement:

"Limiting television viewing time of young children will result in increased reading comprehension skills."

- _____ library catalog
- _____ journal index
- _____ abstract
- _____ bibliography
- _____ Internet resource
- _____ knowledgeable person (subject-matter expert)
- _____ reference librarian

ANALYZING YOUR RESPONSES

While all of the resources listed above are likely to provide useful information, a few will yield the best search results. For primary sources, search in journal indexes and abstracts to locate results of research on reading comprehension and television viewing. An Internet search may result in locating preliminary results of research in progress. You may also be able to communicate by electronic mail with the researcher. To correspond with experts on the topic, you may consider joining a Usenet newsgroup that focuses on reading.

ADDITIONAL RESOURCES

Booth, Wayne, et al. *The Craft of Research*. Chicago: U of Chicago P, 1995.

Campbell, David R., et al. *The Student's Guide to Doing Research on the Internet*. Reading: Addison-Wesley, 1995.

Ellsworth, Jill. *The Internet Unleashed 1997*. Indianapolis: Sams, 1997.

Garrido, Maria Garrido. *Learning Guide to Research on the Internet*. Alameda: Sybex, 1997.

Harris, Cheryl. *An Internet Education: A Guide to Doing Research on the Internet*. Belmont: Wadsworth, 1996.

Levine, John R. *The Internet for Dummies Quick Reference*. 3rd ed. Indianapolis: IDG, 1997.

Maloy, Timothy K. *The Internet Research Guide*. New York: Allworth, 1996.

McKim, Geoffrey W. *Internet Research Companion*. Indianapolis: Que, 1997.

Rodrigues, Dawn. *The Research Paper and the World Wide Web*. Englewood Cliffs: Prentice, 1997.

Wiggins, Richard W. *The Internet for Everyone: A Guide for Users and Providers*. New York: McGraw, 1994.

READING

IN THIS CHAPTER YOU WILL
LEARN ABOUT

- reading sources critically to select the information you need and evaluating the accuracy, reliability, and usefulness of these sources

It is a primary concern for all researchers that not all sources are equal in quality and usefulness. Developing the ability to recognize the best kind of information sources to use to answer your research question is crucial to the success of your paper. Skillful reading of your sources is the best way to ensure that you choose the most appropriate information to include in your paper.

For most of us, reading is a common, daily activity that we rarely think about as we do it. But reading for the purpose of conducting research and completing a source-based writing project is a more specialized and complicated activity that merits closer attention. Reading source material proficiently requires certain skills and prior knowledge that the author assumes of the reader. This section identifies some of those skills and the kind of preliminary knowledge you may need to acquire in order to read your sources efficiently and critically.

THE LANGUAGE OF A DISCIPLINE

Reading as part of conducting research in an academic discipline is a critical and in-depth activity that requires engagement with the ideas and language of the documents you read. Andrea Lunsford and Robert Connors, well-known writing teachers and authors of *The St. Martin's Handbook*, assert that research "calls for active, aggressive reading. Active readers engage in a conversation of sorts with the books they read, responding to them with questions and comments" (590). At the graduate level of study, that "conversation" often involves learning and using a specialized language that is characterized by terminology and ideas familiar to researchers and scholars in a specific discipline.

Every discipline has its own terminology that is understood and used by those familiar with that discipline. For example, biologists use recognized terms such "natural selection" and "adaptability" to describe specific biological processes or phenomena that they wish to discuss or explain. To adequately understand a biology research report or similar document requires a reader to be familiar with such terms and how they are used. Ultimately, this familiarity with the specialized language — or "discourse" — of a field enables a reader to read a text in that field critically in the same way that a classical musician might read a musical score or an art expert might view a painting.

In order to identify, understand, evaluate, and use information and ideas from the sources you gather, you must become somewhat familiar with the language of the discipline or disciplines in which you are working.

In many cases, gaining familiarity with the language of a discipline is simply a matter of reading a variety of texts in the discipline and paying close attention to how the terms and concepts that recur in those texts are used. Sometimes it means actively seeking definitions or explanations for those terms and concepts. For instance, the term "ethnography" is common among anthropologists and sociologists. Anthropologists and sociologists assume that the reader knows what "ethnography" means. A reader who doesn't understand this term and how it is used risks misunderstanding the material.

Similarly, the language of a discipline may include symbols that represent words or processes. For example, Σ (the Greek letter "sigma") means "the sum of" or "add them up." If you are unfamiliar with symbols used in research and statistics, you may be unable to understand the findings reported in a study. In such a case, you must become familiar with these symbols by reading an introductory research methods textbook, searching a comprehensive dictionary, consulting someone with expertise in the field, or attending an introductory course on the subject.

EVALUATING PRINT SOURCES

You will probably need to examine many different kinds of sources in order to find the information you need. Clearly, it would be impossible to read every potential source thoroughly before deciding whether it will be useful. You will have to make decisions about which sources to read thoroughly and which are likely to be relevant for your purposes. You can make those decisions with greater confidence by examining specific aspects of a source. The following list includes some of those characteristics that you should consider when examining conventional published source material (online sources are discussed separately) (Lunsford and Connors 589):

- **Relevance:** Is the source closely related to your research question?

- **Author's credentials:** Who is the author? Is he or she an expert on the topic? Is he or she well known? Have you encountered this author's work before in your research?

- **Date of publication:** How recently was the source published? Is it current? Some sources only a few years old can be out of date if there have been important recent developments in a field. Conversely, some older sources remain standards in a field.

- **Publication background:** Who published the book? Was it published by a respected academic press well known in the field? Was it published by a government agency or a corporation involved in research in the field? Often, publication by a specific agency or company can mean that the text is slanted toward a particular viewpoint on an issue. Academic publications can also exhibit such a slant, but they usually involve rigorous evaluation by professionals in the field before publication.

- **Audience:** For whom was this text intended? Was it written for an audience of experts in the field or for general readers? Often, texts intended for general audiences can be less useful for a research project since such texts may leave out specialized information that general readers may not be interested in.

- **References:** Have you seen references to this text in other publications? Does the list of references in the text include titles you have come across elsewhere in your research? Often, the references can tell you much about how valuable a document will be for your project. If the references include important articles or books that you have come across elsewhere in your research, that's a sign that the source is likely to be useful to you. The list of references can also help you find additional sources for your project.

Lunsford and Connors suggest examining the following aspects for more in-depth evaluation of a source (590):

- **Subtitles:** Titles can sometimes be misleading, but subtitles can often give you a better idea of what an article or book contains.

- **Copyright page:** A book's copyright page can give you a quick picture of the book's publishing history: original date of publication, subsequent editions, and so on. Such information can help you determine the book's usefulness for your project.

- **Abstract:** An abstract is a concise summary of an article or book. In many professional journals, abstracts always accompany the full article; bibliographic databases (such as ERIC) include abstracts along with other publishing information. Abstracts can quickly give you a good idea of what you'll find in a source and can be very helpful as you decide whether a source is worth using.

- **Table of Contents:** The table of contents of a book can tell you a great deal about what you'll find in it. The table of contents in a journal can give you a good sense of the kind of journal it is and help you decide whether the articles within it are likely to be useful to you.

- **Preface or foreword:** These opening pages of a book often provide a clear and relatively detailed picture of what you'll find in the book, the author's perspective, the intended audience, and so on.
- **Index:** A quick look at the index at the back of a book will tell you what major ideas, concepts, and information you will find in that book.

Obviously, the point of examining such characteristics of a potential source is to help you determine relatively quickly whether the source is likely to be useful in your research. As you read through various sources on your topic, you will become familiar with specific ideas and information and even with specific books or articles that are routinely cited by scholars or researchers in that field. You will probably begin to recognize important authors as well. You will also become familiar with the language of the discipline as described earlier. This familiarity will usually help make your research go more smoothly and quickly. But keep in mind that research can be a complicated process, especially when you're entering unfamiliar territory. You need to allow for some surprises and unexpected findings.

EVALUATING ONLINE SOURCES

The previous chapter described many online sources accessible via the Internet and World Wide Web. Although many of the characteristics listed above for conventional print sources also apply to online sources, you may have to approach online sources with some care and evaluate them somewhat differently than you evaluate conventional sources.

First, keep in mind that anyone with a computer and modem can launch a site on the World Wide Web or publish material on the Web and the Internet. Unlike conventionally published books and journals, sites on the Web and the Internet are not necessarily subjected to rigorous peer review or the careful editing process practiced by most academic and commercial publishers.

Second, because the World Wide Web and the Internet are constantly changing and growing, and because they are not yet standardized in the way that conventional print publishing is, sites that you access one week may change or disappear the next. Therefore, it's important to try to determine the relative stability of online sources.

In evaluating online sources, consider the following questions (adapted from *Working the Web* by Carol Lea Clark):

- **Who sponsors the Web or Internet site?** Many sites are sponsored and maintained by professional organizations and thus have the same measure of credibility enjoyed by those organizations. Such sites are usually reliable. For example, the American Educational Research Association (AERA) maintains an extensive Web site that includes searchable bibliographies. AERA is a large, reputable organization that is respected by researchers and scholars in the field of education; its Web site carries the same credibility and can be considered as reliable as the organization's conventional sources. Similarly, organizations such as the American Heart Association and the National Science Foundation maintain Web sites that are essentially online extensions of those organizations and can thus be considered relatively reliable. At the same time, Web sites for interest groups such as the Heritage Foundation, People for the American Way, or the National Organization of Women should be seen as reflecting the political viewpoints of those organizations and approached accordingly. Obviously, commercial sites should be approached with the same critical eye.
- **What are that author's or sponsor's credentials?** The Web contains thousands of sites maintained by individuals, some of whom are affiliated with identifiable and reputable organizations and some of whom are not. If you cannot identify the credentials of the author or sponsor, be wary of the site's credibility.

- **What are the criteria for including information on the site?** If the site contains links to databases, information, and/or texts, try to ascertain how those sources were selected. For example, the site of a professional organization such as AERA might include links to online scholarly journals sponsored by that organization. In such a case, any texts available at the site would have the same credibility as an article published in a conventional scholarly journal. Conversely, some sites include texts written by an individual and "published" on the Web without being subjected to any peer review or editorial process. Such texts may have been published for the author's own purposes and should be evaluated with this in mind.

It is important to note here that the World Wide Web now includes many online scholarly journals. Some of these journals are online versions of the conventional print journals and can be considered just as reliable as the print versions. Other journals are available only on line and represent new forms of publication for scholarship and research. If you are considering using a text from an online journal as a source for your project, you should try to determine whether the journal is peer-reviewed and whether its editorial board is reputable. If information on peer review is not available in the online version of the journal, consult the print version or contact the editor.

In short, the World Wide Web and the Internet contain a wealth of potential source material, but that material must be evaluated carefully. You may need to do extra searching to determine the quality and credibility of information you gather from such sources. Carol Lea Clark sums up the need to be critical about online sources in this way: "One of the revolutionary aspects of the Web is that individuals and organizations are able to put their side of the story directly before the public. It is part of your job as a Web consumer to evaluate critically the motivation or validity of these direct-to-the-public texts" (51).

<aside>
For a thorough discussion of evaluating online sources, visit http://www.library.cornell.edu/okuref/research/evaluate.html.
</aside>

RECONSTRUCTING CONTEXT

Reconstructing context is the process of identifying the circumstances under which an article, study, or essay was written. Every book, article, and study reflects to a greater or lesser extent the attitudes, both public and professional, of the time in which it was written. Especially if you are using older source material, it is crucial that you try to understand the context within which the piece was written. Specifically, you should consider the following:

- **Author's profession or area of expertise:** Does the author have an identifiable bias for or against the topic?

For example, you may consider that an author who works for an HMO and writes about the many ways that HMOs help people and society may have a bias in favor of HMOs. Often, however, an author's bias may be less noticeable. In such cases, your own familiarity with a field and its language will help you identify an author's stance and critically evaluate the source. For example, a scholar interested in literacy may present an interpretation of data on literacy rates that seems straightforward but is actually controversial among literacy experts. A general reader may be unaware of the controversy and thus accept the interpretation as factual. However, a familiarity with some of the literature in the field would enable a careful reader to identify the author's bias.

- **State of the issue at the time of writing:** What was the state of the issue in the culture at large at the time the article or book was published? Was there an accepted opinion or value? Since popular and professional opinions about an issue can change over time, it's important to consider how an issue might have been viewed when the author was writing.

For example, consider how Americans' attitudes toward nutrition have changed in the past several decades. A study on the dietary habits of American adults conducted forty years ago may yield different results than the same study conducted today, since most Americans were unaware of the effects of cholesterol and fat on heart disease at that time. Similarly, an article written about dieting in the late 1970s is likely to reflect certain views about nutrition that may no longer be considered valid by the culture at large.

Prevailing attitudes in the society at large toward an issue may also affect how an author treats the issue. For example, an article written about Russia during the Cold War era may have a very different tone from an article written about Russia today.

EVALUATING CLAIMS

Determining the validity and usefulness of a source is the first step in the process of deciding whether and how to use that source for your project. Even after you've determined that a source is valid and useful, however, you still need to evaluate the claims an author makes. Every piece of writing, even a scientific report, reflects a viewpoint or makes an argument. As you review a source, you need to identify and evaluate that viewpoint or argument by considering the following questions:

• What is the author's main point?

• What evidence does the author present in support of that point?

• Is that evidence persuasive?

• What counterarguments can be mustered?

• Is there any noticeable lapse in the author's reasoning?

• Have you come across other sources that might refute or call into question the author's viewpoint or argument?

As you review your various sources, you may encounter disagreements among them. Keep these disagreements in mind as you decide whether and how to use a source for your project. Some authors may present viewpoints or arguments that are generally accepted by other scholars in their fields, whereas others may present decidedly unique and/or unconventional or controversial viewpoints or arguments. Being able to identify such opposing viewpoints or arguments can ensure that you will use your sources accurately and appropriately.

PLAUSIBILITY

Up to this point we have been discussing the many considerations that you might take into account as you review material for your research project. There are several ways to make these many considerations manageable as you evaluate your sources. Researcher Bill Hord offers one such way. He suggests three considerations that should be made when evaluating a source: (1) external plausibility, (2) internal plausibility, and (3) practical criteria. The following questions are adapted from his online researching guide.

EXTERNAL PLAUSIBILITY

External plausibility measures the credibility of source material.
Consider these questions:

• What are the author's credentials?

• What are the publisher's credentials?

• Who is the intended audience? (The academic community? The general public? A conference group?)

• Has the author documented the sources of his or her information?

• Does the source have any special features that might speed your research or be particularly relevant to your topic?

For Bill Hord's complete discussion of internal and external plausibility, visit http://www.hccs.cc.tx.us/ system/Library/Center/ Reading/ReadAG.html.

INTERNAL PLAUSIBILITY

Internal plausibility measures the fitness of a source for your research project. Consider these questions:

- What is the scope of the source? (What has the author contributed that can't be found somewhere else?)

- Is the information timely? (If you are looking at a book, check the original copyright, not the reprint date.)

- Is the information reliable? (Can you test for this?)

- Is the information valid? (Can you test for this?)

- What is the author's purpose? (To dispute an argument? To make an argument?)

PRACTICAL CRITERIA

Practical considerations concern your ability to acquire and use a source. Consider these questions:

- Is the source available for use in the time given? (Does your library have the source? If not, will you be able to get it through interlibrary loan within the time frame required?)

- How much prior knowledge is required to use this source? (Do you have the background knowledge required to understand the argument made in the source? Are you able to comprehend the argument?)

EVALUATING EMPIRICAL RESEARCH

Empirical research is an original study that attempts to investigate or explain phenomena. A common example of such research is the kind of medical study often referred to in news reports about important medical breakthroughs. For instance, if you hear a report on the news about a study published in the *New England Journal of Medicine* showing a link between colon cancer and a high-fat diet, chances are that report is referring to an empirical study that was published in that journal.

Empirical research reports are based on certain assumptions and conventions regarding how studies should be conducted and reported. Although these assumptions and conventions can vary from one discipline to another, most researchers follow certain general procedures when reporting their research, regardless of their discipline. For example, although a cognitive psychologist studying memory loss and a biochemist studying enzymes associated with memory loss use very different techniques to conduct their research and gather their data, they report the results of their studies in similar ways according to conventions that govern research generally. Both, for instance, include discussions of the relevant literature on their research question, justifications for their studies, detailed descriptions of the procedures they used to gather and analyze their data, and conclusions about what their results mean.

As you read empirical research reports, you will become more familiar with these reporting conventions and will be able to read such reports with increasing efficiency. For instance, you will know where to find the results and conclusions in a study, and you will be able to evaluate the quality of the methods used to gather data more quickly.

Empirical research reports represent slightly different challenges for you as you gather materials for your paper. Since empirical research reports may be significant sources for some research papers that you will be asked to write in your graduate program, it is important to be able to evaluate their validity.

Following is a series of questions adapted from ones by L.R. Gay designed to help you evaluate each section of a formal published empirical research report.

INTRODUCTION

PROBLEM

- Is there a statement of the problem?

- Can the problem be investigated through the collection and analysis of data?

- Is background information on the problem presented?

REVIEW OF THE LITERATURE

- Is the review comprehensive?

- Are the cited references relevant to the problem?

- Are the sources mostly primary?

- Does the review conclude with a brief summary of the literature and its implications about the problem?

THESIS STATEMENT

- Does the research report list the questions the author is trying to answer?

- Does each thesis statement describe an expected relationship or difference between two variables?

- Is each thesis statement testable?

METHOD

SUBJECTS

- Is the method of selecting a sample clearly described?

- Are the size and major characteristics of the population studied described?

- Is the sample size appropriate?

- Was the entire population studied?

INSTRUMENTS

- Is a rationale given for selection of the instruments used?

- Is each instrument described in terms of purpose and content?

- Is evidence presented that indicates that each instrument is appropriate for the sample under study?

- Is validity/reliability of each instrument discussed?

- If the instrument was specifically developed for the study, are administration, scoring, and interpretation procedures fully described?

DESIGN AND PROCEDURE

- Is the design appropriate for testing the thesis statement?

- Was a pilot study conducted? Was it described?

- Are control procedures described?

RESULTS

- Are appropriate descriptive statistics presented?
- Was every thesis statement tested?
- Are the results clearly presented?
- Are the tables and figures organized and easy to understand?
- Are the data in each table or figure described in the text?

DISCUSSION

- Is each result discussed in terms of the thesis statement to which it relates?
- Are recommendations for future action or research made?

Obviously, you may not have enough time for such an in-depth evaluation of every source you encounter. But it is crucial that you develop a critical eye as you gather and review material for your research.

It is also worth noting that at this point in the process of researching and writing your paper, you may find it necessary to adjust, rethink, revise, or even abandon your original research question or thesis. Sometimes the search for and the reading of potential sources bring to light problems with your research question or thesis, or perhaps they encourage you to see the issue you're researching in a new light. They could also encourage you to go in a slightly different direction with your research. If, as you conduct your research, you find that you need to make adjustments or even reject your original question or thesis, that's fine. In fact, it's a sign that you're conducting your research properly: you're engaging in an in-depth inquiry that is leading you to new ideas and new ways of understanding the issues you're exploring. Before abandoning your original focus, however, you should consult your professor, advisor or mentor to determine the most appropriate next step.

PRACTICE EXERCISE

CONSIDERING THE OPTIONS

Find a research report or a journal article on a topic related to an assignment you are working on or plan to pursue (you might try to locate a suitable text on the World Wide Web) and subject it to the questions earlier in this chapter about evaluating source material. Determine how well the paper or article measures up to the standards reflected by the questions.

ADDITIONAL RESOURCES

Bieger, George R., and Gail J. Gerlach. *Educational Research: A Practical Approach.* Albany: Delmar, 1996.

Calishain, Tara. *Official Netscape Guide to Internet Research: For Windows & MacIntosh.* Research Triangle Park: Ventena, 1996.

Hennings, Dorothy Grant. *Reading with Meaning: Strategies for College Reading.* 3rd ed. Englewood Cliffs: Prentice, 1996.

Maker, Janet, et al. *Academic Reading with Active Critical Thinking.* Belmont: Wadsworth, 1995.

McCarthy, Mary-Jane, et al. *Reading and Learning Across the Disciplines.* 2nd ed. Belmont: Wadsworth, 1996.

Wassman, Rose, and Lee Ann Rinsky. *Effective Reading in a Changing World.* 2nd ed. Englewood Cliffs: Prentice, 1996.

CHAPTER IV

ORGANIZING

IN THIS CHAPTER YOU WILL
LEARN ABOUT

- taking notes on what you read so that you can capture the data and thoughts accurately and concisely

- documenting the sources you use so that others can verify your arguments and conclusions

- preparing an outline of the first draft of your research paper

Once you have determined what sources to use for your research paper, read your material, and taken your notes, you must organize your material so that you can most effectively present it to the reader. A carefully organized paper will be more understandable to your reader and will communicate the outcomes of your research clearly and effectively. This section addresses how you can gather the information and data you need from your sources to begin writing your paper.

CREATING AN OUTLINE

After conducting preliminary research and reading, begin organizing your research paper by creating a preliminary outline. Creating an outline will help you organize your ideas and present them in a logical order. It will also help you stay focused when you begin drafting your research paper. You should use your outline as a guide and change it if necessary as you write your paper.

THE OUTLINE

Although many instructors require their students to submit outlines, many writers do not find them necessary or useful. However, when you are writing a complex, source-based research paper, creating an outline can be an indispensable way to organize your material. It can help you keep your draft focused and present your ideas in the most effective way possible.

There are few hard-and-fast rules governing what an outline should include or what form it should take. You should use whatever form is helpful to you as you begin gathering your materials and collecting your thoughts in preparation for writing your paper. Keep in mind that you may need to change your outline as you develop it or as you write your rough draft.

The following suggestions may help you prepare the preliminary outline for your argumentative paper.

- Identify the main argument you wish to include. Then identify any secondary arguments.

- Group the arguments that are related.

- Order the secondary arguments from general to specific, or from abstract to general, or in any other logical way that will help you present them persuasively to your reader.

- Write headings and subheadings reflecting the main points of your paper.

For example, imagine that your research question is "Does the amount of television viewing affect reading comprehension in beginning readers?" and your thesis statement is "Reduced television viewing time results in increased reading comprehension scores in beginning readers." Your preliminary outline may look something like the following outline.

> THE PROBLEM OF TELEVISION VIEWING
> - amount of time children spend watching TV
> - concerns about excessive TV viewing
>
> MAIN EFFECTS OF TELEVISION VIEWING ON HOMEWORK
> - children choose TV as a preferred activity over reading
> - TV encourages passive rather than active engagement with ideas
> - excessive TV viewing leaves children less experienced with written language
> - TV is a negative influence on children's values

It is important at this point to remind yourself about the nature of the writing process. While it is useful to discuss writing in phases, stages, or steps, academic writing is rarely conducted in a strictly linear fashion. Rather, it is usually done, particularly at the graduate level and beyond, as a process involving irregular loops, or cycles: thinking, writing, researching, reading, rethinking, rewriting, researching further, rewriting, and so on.

CORRELATION BETWEEN TELEVISION VIEWING AND PERFORMANCE IN READING AND OTHER ACADEMIC SKILLS

- educators' concerns

- effects of TV on classroom behavior

- relationship between TV viewing and reading test scores

PARENTAL CONTROL PROBLEMS AND BENEFITS

- kinds of control available to parents

- effects of control (especially the amount of control and the type of TV viewing in question) on reading test scores

- suggestions for parents

Note that the headings and subheadings in this example are very broad and refer to general ideas or points that the writer will discuss in the paper. You should be as general or as specific in your outline as is appropriate for your needs. But keep in mind that what is most useful about an outline is that it can help you keep track of the main sections of the paper.

In your own outline, you may find it helpful to include brief sentences or even paragraphs containing summaries of what you intend to write in each main section. It may also be a good idea to include your research question or your thesis statement in your outline to remind yourself of the focus of your whole paper.

Finally, it may be helpful to include references to specific sources in each section of your outline. Doing so may help you envision where you might use the sources in your paper and may make the writing of the draft easier since it will decrease the time you will spend looking for sources as you write.

PRACTICE EXERCISE

CONSIDERING THE OPTIONS

The outline for a paper on television viewing that appears earlier in this chapter is for an argumentative paper. How might an outline of an analytical paper on the same topic look different?

Taking Notes and Documenting Sources

You must now begin extracting information and data from your sources. Since you cannot (and may not want or need to) copy everything verbatim, you should write down only the information that is relevant to your purpose. And you *must* document your sources; that is, you must identify where your information came from.

Taking notes

Take notes on every source that you consider relevant to your research question. Remember to use the interpretation and evaluation tips covered in Chapter III: **Reading**.

The purpose of note taking is to extract from your sources the information that answers your research question or supports your thesis statement. There are three typical formats in which to record notes.

- quotations

- paraphrases

- summaries

You will probably use all three of these formats when writing your paper. More information about using these formats is provided in the section on documenting sources that follows.

Using note cards

Many people take notes on note cards. There are several advantages to using note cards to organize your research notes.

- First, you will write the bibliographic material on each note card. When it comes time to create your bibliography, you can alphabetize the note cards to quickly create the bibliography.

- Second, if you write a single argument, point, or idea on each note card, you can organize your note cards to match the order of discussion topics in your preliminary outline.

- Third, note cards are easy to reorganize. You can easily change the location of an argument or idea within the organization of the research paper outline.

Using note cards is not necessarily required, of course. Some people find that using notebooks or looseleaf binders works just as well for them, and many students use computers for both outlining and note taking. Whatever you use, the point is to have an efficient and organized method to record and access the information you need once you begin writing your paper.

Documenting sources

One of the hallmarks of a good research paper is evidence of the writer's appropriate and proficient use of source material. Earlier sections of this guide explained how to find and evaluate sources as you gather ideas and information for your paper. Incorporating information from those sources into your draft and acknowledging the sources are indispensable steps in writing an effective research paper.

A thorough discussion of plagiarism and how to avoid it can be found in Lynn Quitman Troyka's Simon & Schuster Handbook for Writers *(4th ed.), pp. 518-536.*

Documenting your sources is mandatory in research papers. If you use someone else's ideas or words without giving that person appropriate credit, you are guilty of plagiarism. Whether committed deliberately or unintentionally, plagiarism is a serious offense. You should familiarize yourself with the guidelines regarding plagiarism that your professor or institution utilizes. In general, you must document any instances of the following in your paper:

- direct quotes

- paraphrased opinions of another

- facts or results of a study

As you take notes, you should record the following key information about each of your sources:

- author's name
- title of article, book, paper, or other document
- publisher
- place of publication
- volume (if the source is a periodical)
- span of pages
- copyright or publication date

In addition, if you record a direct quote, paraphrased opinion, or the results of a study or experiment, you must note the page number or location where it appears in the original source.

Although it is beyond the scope of this guide to provide detailed instructions on how to summarize, paraphrase, or quote a source, it is crucial that you understand how to do each of these in your academic writing. This guide offers only a few brief examples. If you are uncertain about how to summarize or paraphrase a source, or if you need further review, consult one of the style guidelines discussed below in "Citing Sources."

QUOTATIONS

Quotations use a source's words *exactly*. Use quotations to provide credibility, to support your argument with expert opinion, or when the actual phrasing of the information is as important to your paper as the ideas expressed by the author. When you use quotes, you should copy the source's words exactly as they appear in the original and follow the style guidelines specified for in-text citations. (We use MLA style citations in this guide.)

The following passage is taken from a historical study of the fourteenth century by historian Barbara Tuchman. It is the original source for the examples of accurate and inaccurate use of quotation, paraphrase, and summary presented in this section. (The original passage from Tuchman and the following examples are taken from Gerald Mulderig's *The Heath Handbook*.)

ACCURATE USE OF QUOTATION:
In a given area the plague accomplished its kill within four to six months and then faded, except in the larger cities, where, rooting into the close-quartered population, it abated during the winter, only to reappear in spring and rage for another six months (Tuchman 93).

Tuchman, Barbara. *A Distant Mirror*:
The Calamitous 14th Century.
New York: Knopf, 1978.

INACCURATE USE OF QUOTATION:
In fourteenth-century cities, the plague "rooted into the close population during the winter, only to reappear in spring and rage for another six months" (Tuchman 93).

In this example, the quoted passage in this sentence resembles Tuchman's but it is not a word-for-word reproduction of her text and is therefore unacceptable as a direct quote. The writer of this example has changed the word rooting to "rooted" and has omitted "quartered" and "it abated."

In medieval cities, according to Barbara Tuchman, the plague "abated during the winter" but typically "[reappeared] in spring and [raged] for another six months" (93).

Here, the writer quotes Tuchman's original passage accurately. Note that to make Tuchman's words fit the structure of her sentence, the writer had to change the original text's "reappear" and "rage" to "reappeared" and "raged;" she indicated those changes by putting the substituted words in brackets. This is a common practice when quoting sources in academic writing. (If you are unfamiliar with this practice, consult one of the writing handbooks discussed at the end of this section.) Note also that because the author stated that the quotation was from Tuchman, it was unnecessary to include her name in the citation.

PARAPHRASES

A paraphrase is a rewording of a statement or passage from a source. A paraphrase contains your own words but should preserve the essence of the ideas presented in the source. You use a paraphrase when those ideas are important for your own paper but the precise words of the source are not. You might also want to paraphrase in order to shorten a section from the source that is too long to quote.

To paraphrase, you should read the source and then, without looking at it, write down the gist of the passage from the source in your own words. Go back to the source and check to be sure that you have not misrepresented the ideas presented there. Be sure to cite your paraphrase just as you would cite a quotation, using the required citation format.

INACCURATE USE OF PARAPHRASE:
In a specific area the plague killed its victims in four to six months and then receded, except in big cities, where it declined in the winter, only to reappear in spring and flourish for another six months (Tuchman 93).

In this example, the writer has merely substituted a few different words for words in the source. The structure of the sentence, however, is Tuchman's. Technically, without the quotation marks this is plagiarism, since the writer is presenting Barbara Tuchman's words as his own.

ACCURATE USE OF PARAPHRASE:
In the crowded cities, the plague never completely disappeared; though relatively dormant in the winter, it returned in full force when the weather turned warm again (Tuchman 93).

This writer has captured the exact meaning of Tuchman's passage but has done so in a sentence that is original in structure and diction. The only major words taken from Tuchman are "cities," "plague," and "winter;" such duplication is acceptable, since they are common words for which it would be inappropriate to use synonyms. The point is that the writer uses Tuchman's ideas, giving appropriate credit for those ideas by citing the source, without using Tuchman's language.

SUMMARIES

A summary of a source you have read sums up the points made in the source. (Note that summarizing a source is not the same as summarizing your paper in the conclusion.) Your source summary should be written in your own words but should not include your own ideas or opinions. You should summarize to express the main idea of a source when you do not need to include all of the details from the source material. Generally, summary differs from paraphrase in that it refers to an entire source or a large section of a source (such as a chapter of a book). Keep in mind that a summary is meant to provide the reader with a concise statement of a source's content.

CITING SOURCES

Faculty at the graduate level almost always expect that you know how to use one or more of the MLA, APA, and CBE style formats and that you will follow their conventions in your research papers.

You must follow whatever style guidelines your professor specifies in citing all sources, including Internet sources. The two style guidelines most frequently used are those of the Modern Language Association (MLA) and American Psychological Association (APA). Writers in the sciences and mathematics frequently use the guidelines of the Council of Biology Editors (CBE). If you are not already familiar with these style formats, you should take some time to learn the basic conventions of each of them.

For detailed instructions and additional information about each style, refer to the *Publication Manual of the American Psychological Association*, the *MLA Handbook for Writers of Research Papers*, and *Scientific Style and Format: The CBE Manual for Authors, Editors, and Publishers*. You can find these publications in most libraries and bookstores. In addition, all good writing handbooks include explanations and samples of MLA and APA style for citing sources. Finally, there are many sites on the World Wide Web that offer help in using APA and/or MLA guidelines in your writing. You can search for these sites using one of the search engines described in Chapter II: **Researching,** or you can visit one of the online writing laboratories listed at the end of that chapter. (MLA, APA, and CBE style guidelines are discussed briefly in Appendixes C, D, and E.)

ADDITIONAL RESOURCES

Ballenger, Bruce. *The Curious Researcher: A Guide to Writing Research Papers.* 2nd ed. Needham Heights: Allyn & Bacon, 1997.

Leedy, Paul D., et al. *Practical Research: Planning and Design.* 6th ed. Englewood Cliffs: Prentice, 1996.

Meriwether, Nell W. *12 Easy Steps to Successful Research Papers.* Oakland: NTC, 1996.

Troyka, Lynn Quitman. *Simon & Schuster Handbook for Writers.* 4th ed. Upper Saddle River: Prentice, 1996.

Turabian, Kate L., et al. *A Manual for Writers of Term Papers, Theses, and Dissertations.* 6th ed. Chicago: U of Chicago P, 1996.

CHAPTER V

WRITING

IN THIS CHAPTER YOU WILL LEARN ABOUT

- writing a rough draft of your paper

- evaluating and revising the rough draft, including incorporating feedback you've received from others and editing your paper for problems in style and grammar

Writing your paper is the step in the research process in which you bring all your previous work together. It is an integral part of your inquiry into your topic. It will result in a finished product that will present the results of your study to your reader.

You might not be aware of it, but you are essentially prewriting the draft of your research paper just by thinking about your topic. The momentum you gain from gathering information will lead the way to your making a commitment to an idea you will explore through your writing. Your sense of commitment is very important, as it provides the motivation necessary to complete the later phases of the composing process.

Writing a Rough Draft

Writing the rough draft is, for many people, the most difficult step in the process of writing a research paper. The only way around this difficulty is through it; that is, you begin your rough draft by writing out the ideas and points in your notes. As you work through your rough draft, expect the unexpected: your thesis statement may change midway through the draft, you will probably need to revise some sections of the draft many times, and you may find it necessary to identify additional sources. It can be helpful to set your expectations for the rough draft accordingly. Be flexible. For now, focus on getting the important parts of your paper written in rough form and moving on from there.

FOUR GUIDELINES

Use the following guidelines as you prepare the rough draft for your paper.

1. Do not begin your rough draft until you have prepared your preliminary outline, finished the bulk of your research, organized your notes, and developed a thesis with which you are satisfied. Generally, you should begin writing the draft when you feel confident of what you want to say.

2. Remember that you are writing a rough draft. Focus on supporting your thesis or answering your research question, but keep in mind that the purpose at this stage is to get your ideas written out so that you have a text to work with as you continue to develop your paper. Remember, the rough draft phase is for getting it down, not for getting it finished.

3. Establish a schedule for working on your paper. Many inexperienced writers make the task of writing a paper more difficult by trying to do everything at once. It is usually more efficient — and usually a little easier — to set deadlines for yourself and work to meet them one by one. Successful writers usually find that working on a schedule in this way makes the task more manageable — and the draft more effective.

4. Break up your draft into parts. As you write, try to develop each component of your paper separately. Whether you are writing an analytical or argumentative paper or a report of an empirical study, you must include certain sections (described below) in your paper. It can be helpful to think of these sections as discrete entities and to work on them one at a time. In this way, you can break up the task of completing the entire draft and make it more manageable.

As you refer back to your outline and begin writing your rough draft, keep in mind that every argumentative and analytical research paper includes an **introduction**, a **body** where arguments and analyses are developed, and a **conclusion**.

> *"Rough draft" is an apt term for your paper at this stage: rough because it is unfinished and not polished, and draft because it is a work in progress that will likely change as you continue to work on it.*

THE INTRODUCTION   All the parts of a paper are crucial, but the introduction can be especially important because it sets the stage for the rest of the paper. You might think of the introduction as the section where you frame your discussion to lay out for the reader what your paper will try to do.

An introduction has three main purposes:

* First, to introduce your topic. The introduction prepares the reader for your paper. It should catch the reader's attention. It should also include your thesis statement (as discussed in Chapter I: **Preparing**).

* Second, to provide the context for the analysis, argument, or results of your study. The context should include any background information the reader would find helpful in understanding the subject matter, including historical background, related topics or issues, and, sometimes, definitions of key terms.

* Third, to provide the initial connection between the writer and the reader. This connection is frequently established by the reader's response to the writer's voice. The voice is the personality and tone the writer projects in the paper. It involves the writer's attitude toward the subject of the paper and toward the reader. You answer the question "What is the author like?" by evaluating clues you take from the writer's voice. A writer's voice is established in the introduction and should be consistent throughout the paper. It is an important element in ensuring that the reader will believe and trust what the writer has to say.

There are many ways to accomplish these purposes in academic writing. Five common opening techniques are

1. introductory quotation

2. overview of an issue or controversy

3. anecdote

4. introductory question

5. direct statement of thesis

The following examples illustrate these five ways to introduce your paper (adapted from Behrens and Rosen 48-51). As you review these examples, look for the thesis statement in each example and consider how the writer establishes voice.

1. INTRODUCTORY QUOTATION
"Two cheers for democracy" was E.M. Forster's not-quite-wholehearted judgment. Most Americans would not agree. To them, our democracy is one of the glories of civilization. To one American in particular, E.B. White, democracy is "the hole in the stuffed shirt through which the sawdust slowly trickles . . . the dent in the high hat . . . the recurrent suspicion that more than half of the people are right more than half of the time" (915). American democracy is based on the oldest continuously operating written constitution in the world—a most impressive fact and a testament to the farsightedness of the founding fathers. But just how farsighted can mere humans be? In *Future Shock*, Alvin Toffler quotes economist Kenneth Boulding on the incredible acceleration of social change in our time: "The world of today . . . is as different from the world in which I was born as that world was from Julius Caesar's" (13). As we move toward the twenty-first century, it seems legitimate to question the continued effectiveness of a governmental system that was devised in the eighteenth century; and it seems equally legitimate to consider alternatives.

In this example, note that the use of quotations provides a context for the paper at the same time that it sets the stage for the author's own thesis, which is stated in the final two sentences of the paragraph. (Note also that the author uses the MLA style for citing sources [see Appendix C: **Modern Language Association Style**].)

2. OVERVIEW

The *American Heritage Dictionary's* definition of civil disobedience is rather simple: "the refusal to obey civil laws that are regarded as unjust, usually by employing methods of passive resistance." However, despite such famous (and beloved) examples of civil disobedience as the movements of Mahatma Gandhi in India and the Reverend Martin Luther King, Jr., in the United States, the question of whether or not civil disobedience should be considered an asset to society is hardly clear cut. For instance, Hannah Arendt, in her article "Civil Disobedience," holds that "to think of disobedient minorities as rebels and truants is against the letter and spirit of a constitution whose framers were especially sensitive to the dangers of unbridled majority rule." On the other hand, a noted lawyer, Lewis Van Dusen, Jr., in his article "Civil Disobedience: Destroyer of Democracy," states that "civil disobedience, whatever the ethical rationalization, is still an assault on our democratic society, an affront to our legal order and an attack on our constitutional government." These two views are clearly incompatible. I believe, though, that Van Dusen's is the more convincing. On balance, civil disobedience is dangerous to society.

In this example, the author attempts to provide an overview of the appropriateness of civil disobedience in a democracy. As in the previous example, the final two sentences state the thesis.

3. ANECDOTE

In late 1971 astronomer Carl Sagan and his colleagues were studying data transmitted from the planet Mars to the earth by the Mariner 9 spacecraft. Struck by the effects of the Martian dust storms on the temperature and on the amount of light reaching the surface, the scientists wondered about the effects on earth of the dust storms that would be created by nuclear explosions. Using computer models, they simulated the effects of such explosions on the earth's climate. The results astounded them. Apart from the known effects of nuclear blasts (fires and radiation), the earth, they discovered, would become enshrouded in a "nuclear winter." Following a nuclear exchange, plummeting temperatures and pervading darkness would destroy most of the Northern Hemisphere's crops and farm animals and would eventually render much of the planet's surface uninhabitable. The effects of nuclear war, apparently, would be more catastrophic than had previously been imagined. It has therefore become more urgent than ever for the nations of the world to take dramatic steps to reduce the threat of nuclear war.

In this example, the writer very effectively sets up the paper by relating an incident that has obvious relevance to the topic being discussed (the threat of nuclear war). Using anecdotes in this manner can be an excellent way to draw your reader into your paper and set the stage for your discussion.

4. INTRODUCTORY QUESTION

Are gender roles learned or inherited? Scientific research has established the existence of biological differences between the sexes, but the effect of biology's influence on gender roles cannot be distinguished from society's influence. According to Michael Lewis of the Institute for the Study of Exceptional Children, "As early as you can show me a sex difference, I can show you the culture at work." Social processes, as well as biological differences, are responsible for the separate roles of men and women.

Here, the writer uses a common technique for introducing a paper: posing a question. Using this approach is a very useful way of framing your discussion of the issue you're addressing. Note that here the thesis statement is placed in the final sentence of the paragraph.

5. DIRECT STATEMENT OF THESIS

Computers are a mixed blessing. The lives of Americans are becoming increasingly involved with machines that think for them. "We are at the dawn of the era of the smart machine," say the authors of a cover story on the subject in *Newsweek*, "that will change forever the way the entire nation works," beginning a revolution that will be to the brain what the industrial revolution was to the hand. Tiny silicon chips already process enough information to direct air travel, to instruct machines how to cut fabric—even to play chess with (and defeat) the masters. One can argue that the development of computers for the household, as well as industry, will change for the better the quality of our lives: computers help us save energy, reduce the amount of drudgery that most of us endure around tax season, make access to libraries easier. Yet there is a certain danger involved with this proliferation of technology.

In this example, the thesis statement is presented immediately in the first sentence. This is a very direct way to put your thesis before your reader and then provide some context before moving into the body of your paper.

Note that examples 1-3 are introductions for argumentative papers, while example 4 introduces an analytical paper. Example 5 can introduce either type of paper.

The paragraphs that immediately follow these introductory paragraphs should indicate what the body of the paper will include. In this previous example, for instance, the writer should follow the introductory paragraph with a brief description of the major points that he or she will discuss. This brief description of the main points of the paper serves as a kind of map that will help the reader follow the argument or analysis. The writer can remind the reader of where the discussion is going by referring back to these main points as the discussion moves from one point to the next. This is a good way to keep the discussion focused and well ordered for the reader.

THE BODY

The body of your paper must answer your research question or support your thesis. You should provide examples or evidence in the body to illustrate and/or support your research question or thesis statement.

The content of the body of your paper will depend largely on the type of paper you are writing (analytical or argumentative) and the kind of information you have gathered in your research. The body of an argumentative paper is comprised of the specific points the writer makes to support the main argument and rejoinders to points made against the main argument. The body of an analytical paper is comprised of the writer's assessment of the existing research on a specific topic. Again, it can be helpful to think of the body of your paper in parts and to draft those parts individually.

As you draft the body of your paper, it is a good idea to follow your preliminary outline to keep your draft organized and focused. As you write, however, you may find that some of your assessments or arguments aren't strategically placed to best answer your research question or support your thesis. If you sense that your arguments aren't working well in the order that you have established in your outline, change the order. A draft research paper is a work in progress and requires continuous revision.

Finally, if you find yourself getting stuck as you write the body of your paper, try rereading your research question or thesis statement with these questions in mind:

- Am I still satisfied with my working thesis, or have I developed the body in ways that indicate I must adjust my thesis based on what I have learned?

- Have I done all the research and evaluating of sources I should have done to fully answer my research question or support my thesis?

Sometimes, problems encountered with a rough draft may be the result of a poorly conceived thesis statement. You may find it necessary to rework your thesis before you can complete the rough draft.

THE CONCLUSION   A good conclusion includes a restatement of your research question or thesis along with a summary of the main points of the body of the paper. However, the effectiveness of a conclusion that only does these two things is marginal. Try to enhance your conclusion by doing one of the following:

• Discuss the personal or global significance of your conclusion.

• Discuss the outcomes of your research in terms of how your argument advances, contributes to, or complicates the general understanding of your subject area.

As with introductions, there is no hard-and-fast rule to follow to write a good conclusion. Write whatever seems to work best to wrap up your paper. For example, the conclusions of papers in many social science disciplines frequently include recommendations for further research. Keep in mind that the conclusion is the last thing your reader will remember of your paper.

Even though there are no specific rules for writing good conclusions, there are three guidelines it may be helpful to follow.

• First, do not include any important points in your conclusion that you have not already discussed in the body of your paper. The conclusion is for bringing closure to the discussion at hand and leaving the audience with a clear notion of the significance of the point or points you are making. The conclusion should *remind* the reader of a key point, not introduce a new one.

• Second, do not deviate from the voice you have maintained throughout the paper. Consistency of voice is important in conventional research papers and you should maintain it in your conclusion.

• Third, be wary of including a question in your conclusion, particularly in an argumentative paper. This technique can be provocative (as when it asks the reader to consider an implication of the conclusion), but it can also undermine the decisiveness of a good argument. Before including a question in your conclusion, make certain that doing so is the most forceful way to end your paper.

EVALUATING AND REVISING A ROUGH DRAFT

Once you have a completed the rough draft, you're ready to begin working with that draft in order to make it an effective piece of writing for the specific writing task you're working on. The key to making your writing effective is careful and thoughtful revision. This final section of the guide should help you learn how to evaluate and revise your final draft.

THE WRITING TASK

The most common mistake inexperienced writers make is to think that once they have completed a draft, the major work is done. It's true that your rough draft represents a great deal of work and may in fact include effective writing. But it is in revising your paper that you work your ideas through carefully, organize those ideas into a coherent and efficient structure, and craft your language so that it conveys your ideas clearly and conforms to the conventions appropriate to your writing task. Don't be hesitant to discard sections of your rough draft that you may like but that may be unnecessary, redundant, or irrelevant. Don't assume that any part of your rough draft is in its final form. Approach your draft as if anything in it can be changed or discarded.

You can help yourself evaluate and revise your rough draft by keeping in mind your writing task. The writing task is your purpose in writing the paper. It answers the question "What am I trying to accomplish in the paper?" Effective revision may require several activities in addition to the rewriting itself: rethinking your ideas, reorganizing your ideas, rereading source material, rewriting whole sections of your draft, tinkering with language and style, and correcting errors. Even the most experienced writers occasionally lose sight of their writing purpose as they engage in these activities. To avoid such a problem, remind yourself continuously of your writing task.

Engage in the following activities and thought processes as you work through your draft:

- If you're responding to a specific assignment, go back and review the guidelines and requirements for that assignment. What does the assignment specifically require you to do? Is your draft responding to that assignment? Have you gotten off the track at any point?

- Consider your audience's expectations for the paper. What do they know about your topic? What do you think they'll need to know? Do they have specific expectations about such matters as structure, style, and source materials?

- Consider your own goals for the assignment or project. What are they? Has your draft set you on course to achieve those goals?

Working through such questions as you begin revising your paper will help you stay focused on your writing task. Remember that you are writing to a specific audience for a specific purpose.

GETTING FEEDBACK ON YOUR DRAFT

It is at this stage in the writing process that getting feedback from others can be invaluable in helping you determine how effective your draft is and helping you decide what revisions you need to make to improve it.

Getting helpful comments from readers, however, may not be as straightforward a challenge as it might seem. Here are two things to keep in mind as you prepare to share your draft with others.

> *As you incorporate feedback from others into your draft, you must ensure that the work in your paper is your own. All good writers benefit from feedback, but none use the work of others as their own. Never incorporate the suggestions of others without giving attribution or rewriting their suggestions in your own words.*

- First, be selective in identifying readers for feedback. Find readers whose opinions on your writing you can trust and whose ideas about your writing you will value—even if you disagree with them on some points. Ideally, your readers should be people who understand something about the work you're doing.

For example, suppose you are writing a philosophy paper. Your neighbor may be an electrical engineer who has no interest in formal philosophy and has never read any books even remotely related to that topic. Such a reader may not be able to follow the discussion in your paper closely enough to provide you with useful feedback. By contrast, suppose you have a friend who sells insurance but who studied literature in college. That friend most likely took some philosophy courses and may have experience with the kind of paper you're writing. That person is probably a good reader for your draft.

In some cases, you might want to ask someone who is *not* intimately familiar with your topic to read your draft so that you can determine whether your ideas are expressed clearly for a non-expert. But in most cases, someone with no interest or background in your topic would not make a very effective draft reader.

- Second, plan to get feedback from more than one person. This can help you identify specific strengths and weaknesses in your draft that a single reader might miss, ignore, or overstate. For instance, if three readers all comment that your ending is confusing, it's a pretty good bet that you need to work on that ending. At the same time, two of those readers might miss a problem with a specific point you are making that a third reader can identify. Sometimes, one reader might offer very strong advice for revising your draft that seems unusual or questionable to you. You can balance that reader's views with the views of other readers, even asking them to react to the advice that the first reader gave you.

USING FEEDBACK

Every reader assesses written material uniquely based on background, experiences, and preferences. Because you may get conflicting advice about your draft from different readers, be aware that you can't fully anticipate how they will react to something you wrote. Consider the feedback you receive carefully before deciding whether to revise in ways your readers suggest.

Ultimately, you must decide which advice to accept and which to reject. In thinking about the feedback you receive from several readers, consider those readers and how they read your draft. For instance, a friend who studied literature in college may have specific preferences regarding the style of a paper, and those preferences may conflict with what the assignment asks you to do. In such a case, your friend's advice for revision may be perfectly reasonable but it may not be appropriate for this particular piece of writing.

You can ensure that the feedback you receive from your readers will be helpful to you if you follow a few simple procedures:

- Be sure to explain to your readers the purpose of your draft. Show them the assignment guidelines so that they'll get a good sense of the task.

- Ask your readers specific questions about your draft. For example, you may be concerned about the organization of the draft. In that case, it would be a good idea to ask whether particular parts of the draft seem out of place. Or you may suspect that your explanation of an important idea is unclear. If so, ask your readers whether they understood the section in question, perhaps even asking them to paraphrase their explanations so you can determine whether they really understood it. In short, ask for comments about the issues that are most important to you or that concern you most. If you do, you're more likely to get feedback that you can use in your revision.

• Specify whether you want your readers to ignore particular aspects of the draft. For instance, you may wish them to ignore the introduction and the conclusion and concentrate instead on the body of the paper. Or, you may ask them to ignore the arrangement of the paper and instead pay close attention to your word choice and sentence structure.

• If necessary, ask your readers to clarify their suggestions or comments. It's a good idea to discuss their comments with them in any case, since such discussions will often lead to further advice and feedback.

REVISING YOUR DRAFT

Once you have received feedback on your draft, you are ready to begin revising. At this point you should have several ideas about the strengths and weaknesses of your draft. Most writers resist the tendency to correct minor errors or to ponder individual words and phrases at this stage. You can attend to such matters later.

Donald M. Murray, a writer and well-known teacher of writing, suggests three readings of each draft. Murray reminds writers that doing "revision is not so much a matter of turning failure into success or correcting errors, although both those things will happen, as it is a matter of making the strengths of the draft stronger" (186). He proposes dividing up the complicated process of revision into three somewhat separate readings in order to focus your attention on appropriate issues and make the task more efficient and manageable.

The process begins with a "global" focus on the overall meaning of your draft and moves to an increasingly "local" focus. The first reading focuses on **meaning**. The second reading focuses on **form and structure**. The third reading focuses on **language and style**. Obviously, there may be overlap in focus among these three readings. But it can be extremely helpful to sort out the task of revising in this order.

REVISING FOR MEANING

First, revise for meaning. This involves reading through your entire draft rather quickly. The purpose of this reading is to get a good sense of the meaning of your draft and of how well the draft is working: how it flows, how its sections fit together, how it is structured, how it moves from one section to the next, how its style and voice sound, how its main ideas structure the paper. As you read, consider the following questions:

• Have you accomplished your writing task? Have you ever strayed from your purpose for writing the paper?

• Is the main idea of your draft coming through clearly? Do you think your reader(s) will be able to see your overall point clearly and follow your discussion throughout?

• Do the sections of the draft seem to fit together? Do any sections seem out of place or redundant? Does the text flow logically from one section to the next?

• Is the draft an appropriate length? Do any sections need to be expanded or condensed?

• Is anything missing? Have you left out important information at any point? Are there any gaps in your draft that require the addition of more material?

- Have you supported your contentions and/or conclusions adequately?
- Is there unnecessary or irrelevant material in the draft that can be cut to sharpen the draft's focus?
- Have you used sources appropriately?

After reading the entire draft through with these questions in mind, make some quick notes about what sections you think require the most revision and then return to those sections. Chances are that you will notice during this reading some of the issues that you have already been concerned about and that may have been pointed out by your readers. At this point in the process, it's appropriate to make big changes: moving paragraphs around, deleting or rewriting relatively large passages, and/or adding new material. Keep your overall point in mind and make the changes accordingly.

REVISING FOR FORM AND STRUCTURE

Second, once you're satisfied that these broader issues are successfully addressed and that your draft is working on the level of its overall meaning, read the draft through again, this time focusing on form and structure. At this stage, you should look carefully at each section to ensure that it contributes to the effectiveness of the draft as a whole. It's a good idea to read the draft in sections or chunks, focusing on each and revising accordingly. You should now be concerned about matters such as the introduction and conclusion, the coherence of individual paragraphs, and the transitions between paragraphs and between large sections of your paper. The following questions can help you focus on such matters as you revise:

- Does the introduction set up your topic and draw the reader into your paper?
- Have you defined, explained, and clarified key concepts or ideas?
- Are the paragraphs easy to follow? Does each paragraph have a clear focus and point? Are the sentences in logical order in each paragraph? Does each paragraph contribute to the overall discussion in that section of the paper?
- Is the conclusion an effective summary of the paper that leaves your reader with a strong sense of your point of view?

Once you have worked through this second reading and made the appropriate revisions, your draft should be essentially complete and working more or less as you want it to. All the "global" issues should have been addressed by now. Your main idea should be coming through clearly and the structure of the paper should be solid.

REVISING FOR LANGUAGE AND STYLE

Third, begin working more carefully with the language and style of the draft. At this stage you should polish the draft so that its wording is concise and engaging. Read through your draft sentence by sentence, phrase by phrase, word by word. Considering the following questions should help you do so effectively:

- Does each sentence work well? Are there any sentences that sound awkward or confusing? Are any sentences too long or needlessly complicated?
- Is your writing concise? Can any words or phrases be eliminated to make your sentences clearer?
- Does the writing sound bland or repetitive because sentence structure is not varied sufficiently?
- Are any sentences redundant or unnecessary, simply repeating an idea from a prior sentence?

- Are there any obvious errors in word choice? Have you selected the most precise and accurate words? Have you used the same words too often in ways that will distract the reader? (On the other hand, have you used synonyms where they might confuse a reader?)

- Is verb tense consistent and correct throughout the draft?

- Have you avoided unnecessary jargon? Have you avoided clichés?

- Have you avoided noninclusive language? Are there sentences which may be misconstrued in ways that might offend a reader? (Note: the MLA, APA, and CBE style manuals contain guidelines for inclusive writing. You should follow these guidelines to ensure that your writing conforms to relevant standards.)

The primary goal at this stage is to make your language as clear and efficient as you can. Try to make each word, phrase, and sentence do its job successfully.

SOME ADVICE ABOUT STYLE

As you work through these revisions, be wary of some of the common advice given to writers by pundits and popular handbooks. Some such advice cautions writers to avoid abstract language at all costs and to use more concrete wording instead; it advises writers to eliminate all jargon from their writing. "Keep it simple" is an oft-repeated maxim.

Obviously, such advice can be useful. You should always strive for clarity in your writing, no matter what you're writing about, and in many cases relatively simple, concrete language can help you achieve that clarity. But not always. In some instances, abstract language is not only unavoidable but also preferable. A philosophy paper, for example, may require the use of abstract language to discuss complex or difficult philosophical concepts.

At times, the use of jargon is essential. If you are writing about a specific area of expertise or knowledge that has a terminology familiar to those who work in that field, you will be expected to know and use that terminology. In some cases, words that have common meanings take on very specialized meanings when associated with specific areas of knowledge.

For instance, in philosophy, anthropology, and psychology, the term "social construction" carries with it a range of meanings — some more subtle than others — due to the varied use of that term in the professional literature in those fields. It is jargon, but it is useful and essential professional jargon. A writer can use that phrase very efficiently to refer to a whole body of knowledge that would be extremely difficult to summarize in plainer language. Yet such a phrase might strike a reader who is unfamiliar with those fields as odd or inflated, and that reader may even consider the use of such jargon to be gratuitous and/or pompous. You should use language that is appropriate to your writing task, even if that means using jargon.

EDITING

Many inexperienced writers think of revision as merely correcting errors. But those activities are really editing tasks. To edit is to prepare for presentation. It is the final step in the process of writing your research paper; it is the polishing of the finished product.

Editing is partially a matter of making sure that your paper conforms to the conventions and rules of standard written English. There are many ways to edit your paper. The most obvious is simply to read through your draft carefully, sentence by sentence, and look for errors in spelling, punctuation and capitalization, and grammar such as inappropriate word choice, incorrect word forms, and so on. If you use a word processor, you should use the spell check function to help you identify and correct spelling errors. However, that won't address problems with punctuation and grammar.

The spell check function on word processors and computers can be an extremely useful tool for editing your paper. However, spell checking does not complete your editing task. There is no substitute for reviewing your paper line by line for meaning, form and structure, and language and style.

A good strategy for editing is to read your paper in sections from the conclusion back to the beginning. In that way, you will be less likely to read for content and more likely to be able to focus on individual words and sentences.

The most efficient way to edit is to become aware of your own patterns of errors or problems and to look for those. For example, if you know that you tend to misuse commas in certain ways, you should read through your paper specifically to find those kinds of errors. Similarly, if you're prone to making errors with certain verb forms, you should look specifically for those. The more you know about your own writing, the more easily you can avoid the errors you're most likely to make and the more efficiently you can edit your paper.

In *The St. Martin's Handbook*, Lunsford and Connors list the twenty most common errors (in addition to spelling) encountered in the writing of college students (I— 1-29). It is a good idea to become familiar with these errors and to check to be sure that you are not making them in your own writing.

- Missing comma after an introductory element
- Vague pronoun reference
- Missing comma in a compound sentence
- Wrong word
- Missing comma(s) with a nonrestrictive element
- Wrong or missing verb ending
- Wrong or missing preposition
- Comma splice
- Missing or misplaced apostrophe
- Unnecessary tense shift
- Unnecessary shift in pronoun
- Sentence fragment
- Wrong tense or verb form
- Lack of agreement between subject and verb
- Missing comma in a series
- Lack of agreement between pronoun and antecedent
- Unnecessary comma(s) with restrictive element
- Fused sentence
- Misplaced or dangling modifier
- Its/it's confusion

If you do not understand the items on the above list, consult one of the handbooks referenced in this guide. It is worth noting that many of the errors on the list are considered rather minor and would most likely be missed or overlooked by many readers. At the same time, though, the fewer errors you make in your writing, the less likely it is that your writing will be judged substandard by an academic reader. Errors often distract readers and lead them to judge the quality of your writing as substandard in general. To avoid creating such a perception, edit your paper carefully.

Practice Exercise

Considering the Options

Ask yourself the following questions to most effectively evaluate your research paper.

Introduction

• Did I clearly state the purpose of my paper and discuss how it relates to previous research?

• Did I include my research question and/or my thesis statement?

• Did I provide background information?

Body

• Do all of my arguments support my thesis statement?

• If not, did I discuss my reasons for including arguments that oppose my thesis?

• Have I provided evidence to support each of my contentions?

Conclusion

• Have I included a summary of the main points of the body of my paper?

• Have I discussed the significance of my conclusion?

Overall

• Have I edited my paper thoroughly and effectively?

• Have I cited my sources according to the prescribed guidelines?

ADDITIONAL RESOURCES

Axelrod, Rise B., and Charles R. Cooper. *The St. Martin's Guide to Writing.* 5th ed. New York: St. Martin's, 1997.

Burnham, Christopher. *Writing From the Inside Out.* San Diego: Harcourt, 1989.

Ede, Lisa. *Work in Progress: A Guide to Writing and Revising.* 3rd ed. New York: St. Martin's, 1995.

Fulwiler, Toby, et al. *The College Writer's Reference.* Englewood Cliffs: Prentice, 1996.

Ross-Larson, Bruce. *Edit Yourself: A Manual for Everyone Who Works with Words.* New York: Norton, 1996.

Schwartz, Marilyn. *Guidelines for Bias-Free Writing.* Bloomington: Indiana UP, 1995.

Strunk, William, and E.B. White. *Elements of Style.* 3rd ed. Needham Heights: Allyn & Bacon, 1995.

Zinsser, William. *On Writing Well: An Informal Guide to Writing Nonfiction.* 5th ed. New York: Harper, 1994.

GLOSSARY

Abstract A concise summary of a published source. (18)

Access point A word or phrase shared by two or more entries in a database. (22)

Access tool A resource that directs you to other resources. Some common access tools are abstracts, bibliographies, indexes, and library catalogs. (17)

Analytical research Research that helps you become an expert on a topic so that you can restructure and present aspects of the topic from your own perspective. (2)

Anecdote The relating of an incident that has obvious relevance to the topic being discussed. (52)

Argumentative research Research that helps you present your position on an issue by using information as evidence to support that position. (3)

Boolean Operators Connecting words such as "AND", "OR", or "BUT" that establish a relationship between search terms. (23)

Chronology A written arrangement of events in order of occurrence. (16)

Compilation A collection of information about a single topic. (17)

Controlled vocabulary A method of searching a database that utilizes a limited set of terms listed in the introductory material of the database. (21)

Database A collection of information organized for rapid research and retrieval. (21)

Descriptor A significant word or phrase used to categorize or describe text or other material. (21)

ERIC The Educational Resources Information Center. A database which provides access to education-related articles, abstracts, and conference papers and proceedings. (15)

Empirical research An original study that attempts to investigate or explain phenomena. (33)

External plausibility The credibility of a source. (32)

Free text searching A method of searching a database in which the database lists every instance of the use of a word or words keyed in by the user. (21)

Help In the context of a computer database, a feature that offers assistance in using the database. (22)

Index A list of information, topics, or references available in a publication. (18)

Interlibrary loan service	A service in which a library borrows materials for its patrons from other libraries. (14)
Internal plausibility	The fitness of a source for your research project. (33)
Keyword	A significant word or term from a title or document used as a search term in an Internet query. (22)
Library catalog	A written or electronic enumeration and description of the holdings of a library. (18)
Link	A connection between an item in a hypertext document and another item in that document, another hypertext document, or a computer file. (17)
Literature review	A gathering and investigation of published material related to a research topic. (3)
Primary research	Research in which a researcher conducts an original study to offer insight into a particular topic. (2)
Primary source	An original, first-hand document such as a creative work, research study, diary, letter, or personal interview. (16)
Query	An inquiry that seeks authoritative information. (22)
Reconstructing context	The process of identifying the circumstances under which an article, study, or essay was written. (31)
Reference tool	A print or electronic document that is itself a source of information. (16)
Review article	A formal, written evaluation of one or more publications. (19)
Search engine	A computer program that searches for keywords in files and documents on the World Wide Web and other sources. (20)
Secondary research	Research in which a researcher compiles research conducted by others and applies it to new questions and/or theories. (2)
Secondary source	A comment about or analysis of a creative work or research study, or an interpretation of a diary, letter, or event. (16)
Theoretical article	A paper which draws upon existing literature to advance a new theory or to analyze an existing theory. (19)
Thesis statement	A proposed answer to a research question. A good thesis statement is specific, restrictive, compelling, and referential. (8)
Truncation	The use of a wild card or other symbol to shorten a term in an electronic search. (24)
Voice	The personality and tone a writer projects in a paper. (51)
Wild card	A symbol used in electronic searching which stands for any letter. (24)
World Wide Web	An Internet subnetwork that employs a powerful cross-referencing software technique to link documents by way of hypertext and hypermedia. (23)

Appendix A: Academic Databases

Note: Some of the following databases are available from database services such as FirstSearch, Academic Index, Dialog, and SilverPlatter. Check with a reference librarian to see what databases your library uses.

Arts and Humanities

Avery Index to Architectural Periodicals
Index of the complete collection of architectural periodicals available at Columbia University Getty Art History Information Module.

Discovering Authors
Index of biographies and critical essays on 300 literary authors. Includes biographical and background information on the author, excerpts from critical essays on his/her writings, bibliography of author's works, and a bibliography of sources of information about the author.

Humanities Index/Art Index
Index of journals, yearbooks, and museum publications in art, architecture, music, performing arts, folklore, film, theater, and dance.

MLA Bibliography
Index of over 3,000 journal articles, books, book chapters, and dissertations in the fields of literature, language, linguistics, and folklore.

MUSE
Database of abstracts of musical literature and the Music Catalog of the Library of Congress.

Music Catalog on CD-ROM
Index of music-related books, scores, sound recordings, serials, visual materials, maps, opera librettos, scores, and recordings in the Library of Congress collection.

The Music Index on CD-ROM
Index of literature on all aspects of music as well as book and performance reviews.

Philosopher's Index
Indexes and abstracts from books and journals of philosophy and related interdisciplinary fields. Major source for aesthetics, epistemology, ethics, logic, and metaphysics.

Poem Finder
Index of poetry in English or English translation that has been published in anthologies, single author collections, and periodicals.

Business and Economics

ABI/INFORM
Abstracts and indexes of articles in over 900 business journals.

Business Dateline
Index of articles from newspapers, city business magazines, and wire services on topics such as industry, health, environmental issues, and education.

Business Periodicals Index
Index of over 250 business journals.

EconLit
Index and abstract of over 400 journals, books, dissertations, and working papers related to economics.

Economic Literature Index
Index with abstracts of over 350 scholarly journals, dissertations, and books related to economics.

General Business File
Database covering business and management topics. Includes a linking feature for profiles of over 150,000 companies along with investment analysts' reports on major companies and industries.

CONFERENCE PAPERS AND PROCEEDINGS

ERIC
Index and abstracts of conference papers and proceedings pertaining to education.

Index to Social Sciences and Humanities Proceedings
Index covering conference proceedings in the social sciences and humanities. Proceedings are derived from publisher and society sources, books or series, reports or preprints.

PapersFirst
Index of papers presented at conferences worldwide.

ProceedingsFirst
Table of contents of papers presented at conferences worldwide as well as a list of papers presented at each conference.

EDUCATION

Education Index
Index of 400 periodicals, yearbooks, and monographs pertaining to education.

ERIC
Index and abstracts of over 850,000 documents and journal articles on education research and practice. Print versions are called *Resources in Education* and *Current Index to Journals in Education*. Personal reference services are provided through ACCESS ERIC at 1-800-LET-ERIC.

Library Literature
Index of 220 periodicals and over 600 monographs pertaining to library and information science.

LISA PLUS
Abstracts of the world's literature in librarianship, information science, and related disciplines.

PsycINFO
Index (abstracts provided for most entries) of scholarly literature in psychology. Includes original research, journal articles, literature reviews, reports of surveys, case studies, theoretical discussions, bibliographies, and descriptions of tests and apparatus.

Social Sciences Index
Index of over 350 periodicals in the fields of anthropology, economics, geography, law and criminology, political science, social work, sociology, and international relations.

Sociological Abstracts
Index and abstracts of over 1,900 journals in sociology and related disciplines such as anthropology, demography, education, law, urban studies, race relations, and social psychology.

ENGINEERING AND TECHNOLOGY

ACM Computing Archive
Reviews of nearly ten years of literature from the computing field. Covers whole books, book chapters, conference proceedings, journal articles, dissertations, and technical reports.

Applied Science and Technology Index
Index of over 350 key science and trade journals covering the applied sciences and technology.

Compendex
Index and abstracts of journal articles, technical reports, books, conference proceedings, and conference papers in engineering and related fields.

Computer Select
Index and abstracts of information on computer-related products and topics, including journal articles, product specifications, reviews, technical tips, manufacturers' profiles, and industry news.

INSPEC
Index and abstracts of 4,200 journals and over 1,000 conferences, books, reports, and dissertations in the fields of physics, electronics, electrical engineering, computer science control, and information technology.

Math-Sci DISC
Index and abstracts covering worldwide research in mathematics and the related areas of statistics and computer science.

General Reference

ArticleFirst
Index of tables of contents of over 12,500 journals in most academic disciplines.

Biography and Genealogy Master Index
Index of biographies on over 4 million people from the beginning of time to the present. Over 2,100 volumes of 700 biographical dictionaries are indexed.

Biography Index
Index of over 2,700 periodicals and 1,800 books, including individual and collective biographies as well as juvenile literature.

Consumer's Index
Subject index of magazine articles and government resources on consumer and health topics.

ContentsFirst
Index of tables of contents of recent issues of over 12,500 journals in science, technology, medicine, social science, business, humanities, and popular culture.

Current Contents — Sciences
Information from title pages of journals published in the fields of agriculture, biology and environmental sciences, clinical medicine, engineering, technology and applied science, life sciences, physical, chemical and earth sciences, and social and behavioral sciences.

Current Contents — Social and Behavioral Sciences
Listing of tables of contents of over 1,350 journals in the social and behavioral sciences.

Dissertation Abstracts
Index and abstracts of all doctoral dissertations completed in the U.S. at accredited institutions for the last 150 years. Includes some master's theses and foreign language dissertations.

EUROCAT
Listing of the European Community's complex documentary output. Includes abstracts of legislation and most publications since 1985.

Foreign Broadcast Information Service Electronic Index
Index of the *Foreign Broadcast Information Service Daily Reports,* which contain translations of news reports, radio broadcasts, and government announcements that originate from other nations.

National Newspaper Index
Index of articles from the most recent four years of *The New York Times, Wall Street Journal, Christian Science Monitor, Los Angeles Times*, and *Washington Post.*

Newspaper Abstracts
Index and abstracts of over 25 U.S. and regional newspapers.

Periodical Abstracts
Index and abstracts of 1,600 journals plus the last 6 months of the *Wall Street Journal* and *The New York Times*. Also includes transcripts of more than 80 news-oriented television and radio shows.

Readers' Guide Abstracts
Index of a core list of abstracts from popular magazines.

Readers' Guide to Periodical Literature
Index of articles from 240 popular magazines and *The New York Times*.

WorldCat
Bibliography describing items held at more than 14,000 libraries. Includes a list of books, journals, manuscripts, musical scores, maps, slides, videotapes, and computer data files.

General Sciences

Analytical Abstracts
Index, with some abstracts, of about 1,300 journals related to analytical chemistry. Includes computer and instrumental applications in analysis.

Chemical Abstracts
Abstracts of 2.4 million pieces of the world's primary chemical and chemical engineering literature as well as coverage of related disciplines such as medicinal chemistry, biology, geology, physics, and civil and electrical engineering.

CRC Composite Index
Index of 300 volumes of CRC handbooks focusing on agriculture, biology, biochemistry, chemistry, engineering, physics, materials science, medicine, and toxicology.

General Science Index
Index of about 140 popular science magazines, professional journals, and the Science Section of *The New York Times*.

GEOBASE
Index and abstracts of literature on human and physical geography, cartography and remote sensing, and international development.

GeoRef
Index and abstracts of earth-science references and the index terms that describe them. More than 4,000 journals in 40 languages are included.

Meteorological and Geoastrophysical Abstracts
Index of books, technical reports, and over 250 journals covering world-wide research in meteorology and related parts of astrophysics, hydrology, glaciology, and physical oceanography.

Publications of the U.S. Geological Survey
Index of U.S. Geological Survey reports and maps. Includes references to non-survey publications and reports.

Science Citation Index
Citation index of international science and technology journals that span over 100 disciplines.

TOXLINE
Citations and abstracts of the world's literature in toxicology and environmental and occupational health.

Life Sciences

AGRICOLA
Index of a compilation of materials acquired by the National Agricultural Library and cooperating institutions. Covers literature of agriculture and related disciplines in journals and conference proceedings.

Biological and Agricultural Index
Index of more than 240 periodicals in the range of sciences related to agriculture and biology.

BIOSIS
Index and abstracts of current research reported in biological and biomedical literature.

Cambridge Life Sciences Collection
Index and abstracts of over 5,000 journals, books, serial monographs, conference reports, international patents, statistical and scientific research, and other English and non-English sources.

Environmental Periodicals Bibliography (EPB)
Interdisciplinary database of more than 400 technical and general environmentally related journals.

Environmental Sciences and Pollution Management
Index and abstracts covering key areas of environmental science including toxic hazards, water treatment, and pollution.

Zoological Record
Index of articles in all areas of zoology including behavior, ecology, feeding and nutrition, parasitology, reproduction, zoogeography, and taxonomy.

HEALTH SCIENCES

AIDSLINE
Citations and abstracts of journal articles, conference presentations, books, audiovisual materials, and computer software on the clinical, research, social, economic, and ethical aspects of AIDS.

BIOETHICSLINE (or BIOETHICSLINE PLUS)
Citations of journal and newspaper articles, book chapters, court decisions, bills, laws, and audio-visual materials on ethical, legal, and public policy issues in health care and biomedical research.

CINAHL
Citations and abstracts from over 550 English language nursing and allied health journals and selected other publications.

MDX Health Digest
Citations and abstracts of health articles written in language suitable for the general public.

MEDLINE
Index and abstracts (most articles) of over 3,500 journals in all areas of medicine, including clinical medicine, experimental medicine, dentistry, nursing, and nutrition.

PsycFirst
Index of more than 1,300 journals. Most records have abstracts. Covers scholarly literature in experimental psychology, psychosexual behavior, educational psychology, applied psychology, and sports psychology.

PUBLIC AFFAIRS AND LAW

GPO Monthly Catalog
Catalog of publications of the United States federal government (Government Printing Office).

Index to Legal Periodicals
Index of English language legal and law-related articles, including yearbooks, annual institutes, and annual reviews of works.

Index to United Nations Documents and Publications
Index of current and retrospective United Nations documents and publications.

LegalTrac
Index of over 900 legal periodicals and newspapers dating back to 1980.

PAIS International
Index of the literature of public policy, social policy, and political and social science.

United States Government Periodicals Index
Index of over 170 U.S. government periodicals.

SOCIAL SCIENCES

America: History and Life
Index of over 65,000 journal articles, book and media reviews, and dissertations on the history and culture of the United States and Canada.

Chicano Database
Index and abstracts of bibliographic citations on the Chicano experience compiled by the Chicano Studies Library at the University of California, Berkeley.

Cross-Cultural CD
Database derived from the fields of anthropology, behavioral sciences, and the humanities. Subjects include human sexuality, marriage, family, crime and social problems, old age, death and dying, marriage, childhood and adolescence, socialization, and education.

ERIC
Index and abstracts of over 850,000 documents and journal articles on education research and practice. Print versions are called *Resources in Education* and *Current Index to Journals in Education*. Personal reference services are provided through ACCESS ERIC at 1-800-LET-ERIC.

Historical Abstracts on Disc
Database of *Modern History Abstracts, 1450-1914*, and *20th Century Abstracts, 1914-Present*.

Human Relations Area Files (HRAF) (Electronic-Human Relations Area Files [E-HRAF])
Index and abstracts covering 350 different cultures and focuses on traditional cultures and North American ethnic groups. Covers anthropology, geography, history, psychology, medicine, ethnic studies, fine arts, literature, social work, law, biology, archaeology, and nursing.

Latin American Studies, Vol. 1
Multi-disciplinary citations from the Nettie Lee Benson Latin American Collection (University of Texas at Austin), the *Hispanic-American Periodicals Index* (University of California at Los Angeles), and volume 50 onward of the *Handbook of Latin American Studies* (U.S. Library of Congress).

Latin American Studies, Vol 2
Index and abstracts of bibliographic records, abstracts, and detailed summaries in business, political, legal, social, and economic trends of the entire Latin American region.

PsycFirst
Index of more than 1,300 journals. Most records have abstracts. Covers scholarly literature in experimental psychology, psychosexual behavior, educational psychology, applied psychology, and sports psychology.

PsycLit
Index of over 1,300 journals, in 27 languages, of the world's serial literature in psychology and related disciplines.

Social Sciences Index
Index of a wide area of social sciences including anthropology, area studies, health, economics, geography, gerontology, ethnic studies, police science, political science, social work, sociology and more.

Social Work Abstracts (SWAB)
Index and abstracts on the subjects of child and family welfare, community organization, aging, and homelessness.

Sociofile
Citations and abstracts of journal articles published internationally in the field of sociology and related disciplines.

Sociological Abstracts
Indexes and abstracts more than 1,900 journals covering all facets of sociology and related disciplines.

APPENDIX B: COMMON REFERENCE WORKS

Note: This is a list of the more common reference works found in most libraries. It is not meant to be exhaustive.

ARTS AND HUMANITIES

Art

Encyclopedia of World Art. Ed. Bernard S. Myers. 16 vols. New York: McGraw, 1959-1987.

The Random House Library of Painting and Sculpture. Ed. David Piper. 4 vols. New York: Random, 1981.

Literature

Dictionary of Literary Biography. 181 vols. to date. Detroit: Gale Res., 1978 to date.

American Writers: A Collection of Literary Biographies. Ed. Leonard Unger. 4 vols. to date. New York: Scribner's, 1974 to date.

British Writers. Ed. Ian Scott-Kilvert. 4 vols. to date. New York: Scribner's, 1979 to date.

McGraw-Hill Encyclopedia of World Drama: An International Reference Work. Ed. Stanley Hochman. 2nd edition. 5 vols. New York: McGraw, 1984.

African American Writers. Eds. Valerie Smith and Lea Baechler. New York: Scribner's, 1991.

European Writers. Eds. William TH Jackson, et al. 14 vols. New York: Scribner's, 1983-1991.

Latin American Writers. Eds. Carlos A. Sole and Maria Isabel Abreu. 3 vols. New York: Scribner's, 1989.

Modern American Women Writers. Eds. Elaine Showalter and Lea Baechler. New York: Scribner's, 1991.

The New Moulton's Library of Literary Criticism. Ed. Harold Bloom. 11 vols. New York: Chelsea, 1985-1990.

The Cambridge Guide to Literature in English. Ed. Ian Ousby. Cambridge: Cambridge UP, 1993.

Masterplots: 1801 Plot Stories and Critical Evaluation of the World's Finest Literature. Eds. Frank N. Magill and Dayton Kohler. 2nd ed. 12 vols. Englewood Cliffs: Salem, 1996.

World Authors: 1950-1985. 4 vols. New York: Wilson, 1975-1990.

Contemporary Authors. Detroit: Gale Res., 1962 to date. Irregular.

Music

The New Grove Dictionary of Music and Musicians. Ed. Stanley Sadie. 6th ed. 20 vols. New York: Macmillan, 1980.

The New Grove Dictionary of Jazz. Ed. B. Kernfeld. New York: St. Martin's, 1994.

The New Grove Dictionary of American Music. Eds. H. Wiley Hitchcock and Stanley Sadie. 4 vols. New York: Macmillan, 1986.

The Guiness Encyclopedia of Popular Music. Ed. Colin Larkin. 6 vols. Middlesex: Guiness, 1995.

Philosophy and Religion

A Companion to Ethics. Ed. Peter Singer. Cambridge: Blackwell, 1991.

The Encyclopedia of Religion. Ed. Mircea Eliade et al. 16 vols. New York: Macmillan, 1987.

Man, Myth and Magic: The Illustrated Encyclopedia of Mythology, Religion and the Unknown. Eds. Richard Cavendish and Brian Innes. 21 vols. to date. New York: Marshall Cavendish, 1995 to date.

The Encyclopedia of the American Religious Experience. Eds. Charles H. Lippy and Peter W. Williams. 3 vols. New York: Scribner's, 1988.

BUSINESS AND ECONOMICS

International Directory of Company Histories. Eds. Thomas Derdak and John Simley. 19 vols. to date. Chicago: St. James, 1988 to date.

Encyclopedia of Management. Ed. Carl Hayel. 3rd ed. New York: Van Norstrand, 1982.

Women in the Workplace. Phyllis A. Wallace. Boston: Auburn, 1982.

The ABL-CLIO Companion to Women in the Workplace. Eds. Dorothy Schneider and Carl J. Schneider. Santa Barbara: ABC-CLIO, 1993.

Encyclopedia of Associations. Detroit: Gale Res., 1961 to date. Annual.

Brands and Their Companies. Detroit: Gale Res., 1990 to date. Annual.
(*formerly* Trade Names Dictionary)

The Foundation Directory. New York: Columbia UP, 1960 to date. Annual.

Biographical Dictionary of American Business Leaders. Ed. John N. Ingham. 4 vols. Westport: Greenwood, 1983.

Standard and Poor's Register of Corporations, Directors and Executives. 3 vols. New York: Standard and Poor's, 1928 to date. Annual.

Encyclopedia of American Economic History: Studies of the Principal Movements and Ideas. Ed. Glenn Porter. 3 vols. New York: Scribner's, 1980.

The New Palgrave: A Dictionary of Economics. Eds. John Eatwell and Murray Milgate. 4 vols. London: Macmillan, 1987.

EDUCATION

Encyclopedia of Educational Research. Ed. Marvin C. Alkin. 6th ed. 4 vols. New York: Macmillan, 1992.

The Encyclopedia of Higher Education. Eds. Burton R. Clark and Guy R. Neave. 4 vols. Oxford: Pergamon, 1992.

Encyclopedia of Special Education. Eds. Cecil R. Reynolds and Lester Mann. 3 vols. New York: Wiley, 1987.

Review of Research in Education. American Educational Research Association. Itasca: Peacock, 1973 to date. Annual.

ENGINEERING AND TECHNOLOGY

Encyclopedia of Artificial Intelligence. Ed. Stuart C. Shapiro. 2nd ed. 2 vols. New York: Wiley, 1992.

Encyclopedia of Computer Science and Engineering. Eds. Anthony Ralston and Edwin D. Reilly. New York: Van Norstrand, 1983.

Macmillan Encyclopedia of Computers. Ed. Gary G. Bitter. 2 vols. New York: Macmillan, 1992.

GENERAL AND REFERENCE

Biography
McGraw-Hill Encyclopedia of World Biography: An International Reference Work. 17 vols. to date. New York: McGraw, 1973 to date.

Current Biography. New York: Wilson, 1940 to date. Monthly except December.

Dictionary of American Biography. 10 vols. and eight supplements to date. New York: Scribner's, 1974. (Supplements: 1977 to date)

Dictionary of American Negro Biography. Eds. Rayford W. Logan and Michael R. Winston. New York: Norton, 1982.

Black Women in America: An Historical Encyclopedia. Ed. Darlene Clark Hine. 2 vols. New York: Carlson, 1993.

Notable American Women: (1607-1950). Ed. Edward T. James. 3 vols. Cambridge: Harvard UP, 1971. (Supplements: 1980, 1983)

Dictionary of National Biography. Eds. Leslie Stephen and Sidney Lee. 22 vols. London: Oxford UP, 1938. (Updated by supplements)

Research Guide to European Historical Biography, 1450 to Present. 8 vols. Washington, DC: Beach, 1992-1993.

Great Lives from History: American Series. Ed. Frank N. Magill. 5 vols. Pasadena: Salem, 1987. (note: other series available.)

Countries

Encyclopedia of the Third World. George T. Kurian. 4th ed. 3 vols. New York: Facts on File, 1992.

Worldmark Encyclopedia of the Nations. 7th ed. 5 vols. New York: Wiley, 1988.

Information China: The Comprehensive and Authoritative Reference Source of New China. C.V. James. 3 vols. Oxford: Pergamon, 1989.

The Cambridge Encyclopedia of Latin America and the Caribbean. Eds. Simon Collier and Thomas E. Skidmore. 2nd ed. Cambridge: Cambridge UP, 1992.

The Canadian Encyclopedia. Ed. James H. Marsh. 2nd ed. 4 vols. Edmonton: Hurtig, 1988.

Japan: An Illustrated Encyclopedia. 2 vols. to date. Tokyo: Kodansha, 1993 to date. (*note: updates* Kodansha Encyclopedia of Japan)

The Cambridge Encyclopedia of India, Pakistan, Bangladesh, Sri Lanka, Nepal, Bhutan and the Maldives. Ed. Frances Robinson. Cambridge: Cambridge UP, 1989.

Soviet Union: A Country Study. Ed. Raymond E. Zickel. Washington, DC: Library of Congress, 1991.

Times Atlas of the World: *Comprehensive Edition*. 8th ed. London: Newspapers Ltd., 1990.

Canadian Almanac and Directory. Toronto: Copp Clark, 1948 to date. Annual.

The Europa World Yearbook. London: Europa, 1976 to date. Annual. (*formerly* Europa Yearbook.)

Statesman's Yearbook. New York: Macmillan, 1864 to date. Annual.

National Atlas of the United States of America. US Geological Survey. Washington, DC: GPO, 1970 to date.

Current Issues

CQ Researcher. Washington, DC: Congressional Quarterly, 1991 to date. 48/year.

Facts on File: A Weekly World News Digest With Index. New York: Facts on File, 1940 to date.

Data and Factual Information

World Almanac and Book of Facts. New York: World-Telegram, 1868 to date. Annual.

Information Please Almanac, Atlas and Yearbook. New York: Simon, 1947 to date. Annual.

The People's Almanac. Ed. David Wallechinsky. New York: Doubleday, 1975. (Supplements: 1978 and 1981.)

Statistical Abstract of the United States. Washington, DC: US Bureau of the Census, 1879 to date. Annual.

Historical Statistics of the United States: *Colonial Times to 1970*. 2 vols. Washington, DC: US Bureau of the Census, 1975.

Statistical Yearbook. United Nation's Statistical Division. New York: United Nations, 1993 to date. Biennial.

County and City Data Book. Washington, DC: US Bureau of the Census, 1952 to date. Irregular.

State and Metropolitan Area Data Book. Washington, DC: US Bureau of the Census, 1980 to date. Irregular.

PUBLIC AFFAIRS AND LAW

Encyclopedia of Crime and Justice. Ed. Sanford H. Kadish. 4 vols. New York: Free, 1983.

Congressional Quarterly's Guide to the United States Supreme Court. Ed. Elder Witt. 2nd ed. Washington, DC: Congressional Quarterly, 1990.

Encyclopedia of the American Judicial System: Studies of the Principal Institutions and Processes of Law. Ed. Robert S. Janosik. 3 vols. New York: Scribner's, 1987.

The Guide to American Law: Everyone's Legal Encyclopedia. 12 vols. St. Paul: West Public, 1983. (Annual Supplements, 1990 to date).

Encyclopedia of the American Constitution. Leonard W. Levy. 4 vols. New York: Macmillan, 1986.

Encyclopedia of American Political History: Studies of the Principal Movements and Ideas. Ed. Jack P. Greene. 3 vols. New York: Scribner's, 1984.

Encyclopedia of American Foreign Policy: Studies of the Principal Movements and Ideas. Alexander DeConde. 3 vols. New York: Scribner's, 1978.

Congressional Quarterly Almanac. Washington, DC: Congressional Quarterly News Features, 1948 to date. Annual.

Encyclopedia of The American Presidency. Eds. Leonard W. Levy and Louis Fisher. 4 vols. New York: Simon, 1994.

Congressional Quarterly's Guide to Congress. 4th ed. Washington, DC: Congressional Quarterly, 1991.

Congress and the Nation. Washington, DC: Congressional Quarterly Service, 1965 to date. Quadrennial. (note: volume I includes 1945-1964.)

United States Government Manual. Washington, DC: Office of the Federal Register, 1973 to date. Annual.

SCIENCES

General Science

The New Illustrated Science and Invention Encyclopedia: How it Works. Eds. Donald Clarke and Mark Dartford. 28 vols. New York: Stuttman, 1994.

McGraw-Hill Encyclopedia of Science and Technology. Eds. Sybil P. Parker and Jonathan Weil. 8th ed. 20 vols. New York: McGraw, 1997.

Encyclopedia of Physical Science and Technology. Ed. Robert Meyers. 2nd ed. 18 vols. San Diego: Academic, 1992.

Van Norstrand's Scientific Encyclopedia. Eds. Douglas M. Considine and Glenn D. Considine. 8th ed. 2 vols. New York: Van Norstrand, 1995.

CRC Handbook of Chemistry and Physics: A Ready Reference Book of Chemical and Physical Data. Boca Raton: CRC, 1913 to date. Annual.

Life Sciences

The Marshall Cavendish Illustrated Encyclopedia of Plants and Earth Sciences. 10 vols. New York: Marshall Cavendish, 1988-1990.

Grzimek's Animal Life Encyclopedia. Bernhard Grzimek. 13 vols. New York: Van Norstrand, 1972-1975.

Global Ecology Handbook: What You Can Do About the Environmental Crisis. Global Tomorrow Coalition and Walter Corson. Boston: Beacon, 1990.

The United States Energy Atlas. David G. Cuff. 2nd ed. New York: Macmillan, 1985.

Health Sciences

Encyclopedia of Bioethics. Ed. Warren T. Reich. 2nd ed. 5 vols. New York: Free, 1995.

Medical and Health Annual. Chicago: Encyclopedia Britannica, Inc., 1990 to date. Annual.

The Oxford Companion to Medicine. Eds. John Walton et al. 2 vols. Oxford: Oxford UP, 1986.

The New Our Bodies, Ourselves: A Book by and for Women. Boston Women's Health Book Collective. New York: Simon, 1992.

Physician's Desk Reference to Pharmaceutical Specialties and Biologicals. Oradell: Medical Economics, 1947 to date. Annual.

SOCIAL SCIENCES

Ethnic Studies

Harvard Encyclopedia of American Ethnic Groups. Ed. Stefan Thernstrom. Cambridge: Belknap-Harvard, 1980.

The African-American Almanac. 6th ed. Detroit: Gale Research, 1994 to date. Every three years. (Note: 1st edition titled, *The Negro Almanac: A Reference Work on the African-American.*)

History

Dictionary of Asian American History. Ed. Hung-Chan Kim. New York: Greenwood, 1986.

Dictionary of Mexican American History. Eds. Matt S. Meier and Feliciano Rivera. Westport: Greenwood, 1981.

Great Events from History. Ed. Frank N. Magill. 9 vols. Englewood Cliffs: Salem, 1972-1975.

Dictionary of American History. Ed. Louise Bilebof Ketz. 8 vols. New York: Scribner's, 1976-1978. (Supplement: 1996)

The Reader's Companion to American History. Eds. Eric Foner and John Arthur Garraty. Boston: Houghton, 1991.

Handbook of North American Indians. Ed. William C. Sturtevant. Washington, DC: Smithsonian Inst., 1978-1990.

Encyclopedia of Black America. Eds. W. Augustus Law and Virgil Clift. New York: McGraw, 1981.

Africa South of the Sahara. London: Europa, 1971 to date. Annual.

The Cambridge Encyclopedia of the Middle East and North Africa. Ed. Trevor Mostyn. New York: Cambridge UP, 1988.

Encyclopedia of Asian History. Ed. T. Embree Ainslie. 4 vols. New York: Scribner's, 1988.

The Random House Timetables of History. 2nd edition. New York: Random, 1996.

Macmillan Concise Dictionary of World History. Ed. Bruce Wetterau. New York: Macmillan, 1986.

The Times Atlas of World History. Ed. Geoffrey Barraclough. Maplewood: Hammond, 1989.

Psychology, Sociology, Anthropology

Encyclopedia of Adolescence. Ed. Richard M. Lerner. New York: Garland, 1990.

International Encyclopedia of the Social Sciences. Ed. David L. Sills. 19 vols. New York: Macmillan, 1968-1991.

Encyclopedia of Psychology. Ed. Raymond J. Corsini. 2nd ed. New York: Wiley, 1994.

International Encyclopedia of Psychiatry, Psychology, Psychoanalysis, and Neurology. Ed. Benjamin B. Wolman. 12 vols. New York: Aesculapius, 1978. (note: Progress Volume 1 published in 1983.)

Encyclopedia of World Cultures. Ed. David Levinson. 10 vols. Boston: G.K. Hall, 1995.

The Illustrated Encyclopedia of Mankind. Ed. Yvonne Deutch. 22 vols. New York: Marshall Cavendish, 1990.

Encyclopedia of Sociology. Eds. Edgar F. Borgatta and Marie L. Borgatta. 4 vols. New York: Macmillan, 1992.

Encyclopedia of Homosexuality. Ed. Wayne Dynes. 2 vols. Chicago: Garland, 1990.

The Encyclopedia of Aging. Ed. George L. Maddox. 2nd ed. New York: Springer, 1995.

Women's Studies

The American Woman. New York: Norton, 1996 to date. Annual.
(*formerly* The American Woman: A Status Report.)

Women's Studies Encyclopedia. Ed. Helen Tierney. 3 vols. New York: Greenwood, 1989-1991.

Handbook of American Women's History. Ed. Angela Howard Zophy. Chicago: Garland, 1990.

The Woman's Desk Reference. Eds. Irene Franck and David Brownstone. New York: Viking, 1993.

Appendixes C, D, and E: Guidelines for Citing Sources

The guidelines that follow in Appendixes C, D, and E offer representative samples of three major citation styles: Modern Language Association (Appendix C), American Psychological Association (Appendix D), and Council of Biology Editors (Appendix E). These are the citation styles most commonly used in the humanities, social sciences, and natural sciences and mathematics, respectively.

These guidelines are brief and introductory. They are included here to introduce the three styles, illustrate the differences between them, and direct you to the authoritative style manuals. The style manuals contain thorough information on citing sources. You should obtain a style manual for the citation style required for your research paper.

Appendix C: Modern Language Association (MLA) Style

For thorough information about citing sources using the MLA style, consult the *MLA Handbook for Writers of Research Papers* 4th ed. by Joseph Gibaldi (New York: MLA, 1995). For online information about citing electronic sources using the MLA style, go to *www.uvm.edu/~xli/reference/mla.html*.

In-text Citations in the Modern Language Association Style

1. Paraphrased or summarized source when you mention the author's name
Bergen argues that the information age is no longer coming: it has arrived (1).

2. Short quotation when you mention the author's name
Safire states that "[e]very President can make use of good writing help" (30).

3. Paraphrased or summarized source when you do not mention the author's name
One researcher has even found that dreams move backward in time as the night progresses (Dement 71).

4. More than one source from the same author
One current theory emphasizes the principle that dreams express "profound aspects of personality" (Foulkes, "Sleep" 184). But investigation shows that young children's dreams are "rather simple and unemotional" (Foulkes, "Steroids" 22).

5. Source with no named author
Random testing for use of steroids by athletes is facing strong opposition by owners of several of these teams ("Steroids" 22).

6. Indirect source
Fred Fairchild, a farmer in North Dakota, stated, "If I were of conscription age and had no dependents and were drafted, I would refuse to serve" (qtd. in Zinn 362).

Modern Language Association-Style Works Cited List

1. Book with one author
Thomas, Lewis. *The Lives of a Cell: Notes of a Biology Watcher*. Toronto: Bantam, 1975.

2. Book with two or three authors
Smith, Richard J., and Mark Gibbs. *Navigating the Internet*. Indianapolis: Sams, 1994.

3. Book with more than three authors
Harasim, Linda, et al. *Learning Networks*. Cambridge: MIT P, 1995.

4. Book with no named author
The World Almanac and Book of Facts 1997. Mahwah: K-III Ref. Corp., 1996.

5. One selection from an anthology or collection
Mowatt, Ian and Gerda Siann. "Learning in Small Groups." *Adult Learning: A Reader*. Ed. Peter Sutherland. London: Kogan Page, 1997. 94-105.

6. Book with an author and an editor
Freud, Sigmund. *The Interpretation of Dreams*. Ed. James Strachey. New York: Avon, 1965.

7. Government publication
United States. Dept. of Labor. Bureau of Labor Statistics. *Consumer Expenditure Survey, 1990-91 (Bulletin 2425)*. Washington, D.C.: GPO, 1993.

8. Article in a journal that pages each issue separately
Pritchard, Marietta. "The Rings of Our Grandmothers." *The Massachusetts Review* 37.1 (1996): 121-129.

9. Article in a newspaper
Strout, Richard L. "Another Bicentennial." *Christian Science Monitor* 10 Nov. 1978: 27.

10. Non-periodical information on CD-ROM
Wick, James, and Dave Jackson. *Wayzata World Factbook* 1993, Ed. CD-ROM. Wayzata Tech., 1992.

APPENDIX D: AMERICAN PSYCHOLOGICAL ASSOCIATION (APA) STYLE

For thorough information about citing sources using the APA style, consult the *Publication Manual of the American Psychological Association* 4th ed. (Washington, DC: APA, 1994). For information about citing electronic sources using the APA style, go to *www.uvm.edu/~xli/reference/apa.html*.

IN-TEXT CITATIONS IN THE AMERICAN PSYCHOLOGICAL ASSOCIATION STYLE

1. Paraphrased or summarized source when you mention the author's name
Bergen (1996, p. 1) argues that the information age is no longer coming: it has arrived.

2. Short quotation when you mention the author's name
Safire states that "[e]very President can make use of good writing help" (1997, p. 30).

3. Paraphrased or summarized source when you do not mention the author's name
One researcher has even found that dreams move backward in time as the night progresses (Dement, 1989, p. 71).

4. More than one source from the same author
One current theory emphasizes the principle that dreams express "profound aspects of personality" (Foulkes, 1991, p. 184). But investigation shows that young children's dreams are "rather simple and unemotional" (Foulkes, 1984, p. 22).

5. Source with no named author
Random testing for use of steroids by athletes is facing strong opposition by owners of several of these teams ("Steroids," 1995, p. 22).

6. Indirect source
Fred Fairchild, a farmer in North Dakota, stated, "If I were of conscription age and had no dependents and were drafted, I would refuse to serve" (qtd. in Zinn, 1980, p. 362).

AMERICAN PSYCHOLOGICAL ASSOCIATION-STYLE REFERENCES LIST

1. Book with one author
Thomas, L. (1975). *The lives of a cell: Notes of a biology watcher*. Toronto: Bantam Books.

2. Book with two authors
Smith, R. J., & Gibbs, M. (1994). *Navigating the Internet*. Indianapolis, IN: Sams.

3. Book with more than two authors
Harasim, L., Hiltz, R.H., Teles, L., & Turoff, M. (1995). *Learning networks*. Cambridge, MA: MIT Press.

4. Book with no named author
The world almanac and book of facts 1997. (1996). Mahwah, NJ: K-III Reference.

5. One selection from an anthology or collection
Mowatt, I., & Siann, G. (1997). Learning in Small Groups. In P. Sutherland, (Ed.), *Adult learning: A reader* (pp. 94-105). London: Kogan Page.

6. Book with an author and an editor
Freud, S. (1965). *The interpretation of dreams*. (J. Strachey. Ed.). New York: Avon Books.

7. Government publication
United States, Department Of Labor, Bureau of Labor Statistics. (1993). *Consumer expenditure survey, 1990-91* (Bulletin 2425). Washington, DC: Government Printing Office.

8. Article in a journal that pages each issue separately
Pritchard, M. (1996). The rings of our grandmothers. *The Massachusetts Review, 37*, (1), 121-129.

9. Article in a newspaper
Strout, R. L. (1978, November 10). Another bicentennial. *Christian Science Monitor*, p. 27.

10. Non-periodical information on CD-ROM
Wick, J., and Jackson, D. (1992). *Wayzata world factbook* 1993 Edition [CD-ROM]. New York: Wayzata Technology.

Appendix E: Council of Biology Editors (CBE) Style

For thorough information about citing sources using the CBE style, consult *The CBE Manual for Authors, Editors, and Publishers* 6th ed. (Cambridge: Cambridge UP, 1994).

In-text Citations in the Council of Biology Editors Style

1. Paraphrased or summarized source when you mention the author's name
Bergen (1996, p 1) argues that the information age is no longer coming: it has arrived.

2. Short quotation when you mention the author's name
Safire (1997, p 30) states that "[e]very President can make use of good writing help."

3. Paraphrased or summarized source when you do not mention the author's name
One researcher (Dement 1989, p 71) has even found that dreams move backward in time as the night progresses.

4. More than one source from the same author
One current theory (Foulkes 1991, p 184) emphasizes the principle that dreams express "profound aspects of personality." But investigation (Foulkes 1984, p 22) shows that young children's dreams are "rather simple and unemotional."

5. Source with no named author
Random testing for use of steroids by athletes is facing strong opposition by owners of several of these teams (Steroids 1955, p 22).

6. Indirect source
Fred Fairchild, a farmer in North Dakota, stated, "If I were of conscription age and had no dependents and were drafted, I would refuse to serve" (cited in Zinn 1980, p 362).

Council of Biology Editors-Style References List

1. Book with one author
Thomas L. The lives of a cell: notes of a biology watcher. Toronto: Bantam Books; 1975. 179 p.

2. Book with two authors
Smith RJ, Gibbs M. Navigating the Internet. Indianapolis: Sams; 1994. 267 p.

3. Book with more than two authors
Harasim L, Hiltz SR, Teles L, Turoff M. Learning networks. Cambridge: MIT Pr; 1995. 329 p.

4. Book with no named author
The world almanac and book of facts 1997. Mahwah, (NJ): K-III Reference Corporation; 1996. 975 p.

5. One selection from an anthology or collection
Mowatt I, Siann G. Learning in small groups. In: Sutherland P, editor. Adult learning: a reader. London: Kogan Page; 1997. p 94-105.

6. Book with an author and an editor
Freud S. The interpretation of dreams. Strachey J, editor. New York: Avon Books; 1965. 476 p.

7. Government publication
Department of Labor: Bureau of Labor Statistics (US). Consumer Expenditure Survey, 1990-91 (Bulletin 2425). 1993. Washington: Government Printing Office.

8. Article in a journal that pages each issue separately
Pritchard M. The rings of our grandmothers. The Massachusetts Rev. 1996;37(1):121-9.

9. Article in a newspaper
Strout RL. Another bicentennial. Christian Sci. Monitor 1978 Nov. 10: 27 (col 1).

10. Non-periodical information on CD-ROM
Wick J, Jackson D. Wayzata world factbook 1993 Edition [CD-ROM]. New York: Wayzata Technology; 1992.

WORKS CITED

Behrens, Laurence, and Leonard J. Rosen. *Writing and Reading Across the Curriculum*. 6th ed. New York: Longman, 1997.

Clark, Carol Lea. *Working the Web: A Student's Guide*. Austin: Harcourt, 1997.

Gay, L.R. *Educational Research: Competencies for Analysis & Application*. 3rd ed. Columbus: Merrill, 1987.

Hacker, Diana. *The Bedford Handbook for Writers*. 5th edition. Boston: Bedford, 1998.

Hord, Bill. "The Research Center: A Guide to Using Libraries and other Information Facilities" [Online] (1995) Available URL: *http://www.hccs.cc.tx.us/system/Library/Center/Reading/ReadAG.html*.

Lunsford, Andrea, and Robert Connors. *The St. Martin's Handbook*. 3rd ed. New York: St. Martin's, 1996.

Mulderig, Gerald. *The Heath Handbook*. 13th ed. Lexington: D.C. Heath, 1995.

Murray, Donald M. *Write to Learn*. 5th ed. New York: Harcourt, 1996.

"Writer's Complex." Empire State College. [Online] (1995-1996) Available URL: *http://www.esc.edu/htmlpages/writer/vwcmentxt.html*.